INTRODUCING

CULTURE

Ernest L. Schusky

ASSOCIATE PROFESSOR OF ANTHROPOLOGY
SOUTHERN ILLINOIS UNIVERSITY

T. Patrick Culbert

ASSISTANT PROFESSOR OF ANTHROPOLOGY
UNIVERSITY OF ARIZONA

PRENTICE-HALL, INC., *Englewood Cliffs, New Jersey*

PRENTICE-HALL ANTHROPOLOGY SERIES

David M. Schneider, *Editor*

Printed in the United States of America

Library of Congress Catalog Card Number: 67–17408

PRENTICE-HALL INTERNATIONAL, INC., *London*
PRENTICE-HALL OF AUSTRALIA, PTY. LTD., *Sydney*
PRENTICE-HALL OF CANADA, LTD., *Toronto*
PRENTICE-HALL OF INDIA (PRIVATE) LTD., *New Delhi*
PRENTICE-HALL OF JAPAN, INC., *Tokyo*

NOTE TO INSTRUCTORS

This book is designed to introduce the basic concepts of anthropology and to show how they relate to the concept of culture. Prehistory and physical anthropology are examined only in so far as they contribute to the concept of culture. Even theories and concepts in cultural anthropology have been limited to those which we felt contributed most to an understanding of culture. In short, the book is designed as an elementary, basic introduction to the concept of culture.

We have found that it is most useful in a one-quarter or one-semester course at the freshman or sophomore level. It is sufficiently concise that students can master the terminology with little difficulty. Moreover, it is also possible to supplement this text with other readings. Instructors may assign readings according to their individual taste. For instance, we have used it with parts of Kluckhohn's, *Mirror for Man*; Childe's, *Man Makes Himself*; and Benedict's, *Patterns of Culture*. The book makes no specific reference to other sources within the text so that instructors have complete freedom of choice in selection of supplementary readings. A few annotated references are listed at the end of each chapter for the student who wishes to explore a subject more thoroughly.

In addition to a fast-growing supply of ethnographies and classic writings in paperback form, there are many excellent films to be used in teaching anthropology. Casts of fossil men and stone age implements are likewise available at moderate cost. Information on these new developments may be found in *Resources for the Teaching of Anthropology*, Memoir 95, of the American Anthropological Association. Memoir 94, *The Teaching of Anthropology*, is most valuable for explaining the role of anthropology in the liberal arts curriculum. The instructor without extensive training in anthropology will find these memoirs particularly valuable.

It will soon become obvious to the instructor who uses this book that it serves primarily as a manual for his students. What and how much they learn depends ultimately on the instructor and his ability as a teacher. We feel very strongly that this should be so. Anthropology as a profession has been marked by great teachers, and any history of anthropology notes the influence of one generation of anthropologists on another as a relationship between teacher and student. Credit for any contribution this book makes to the teaching of anthropology should go largely to the authors' professors at the University of Chicago, who were not only firm taskmasters but also firm friends.

E.L.S.

T.P.C.

CONTENTS

ILLUSTRATIONS

1

INTRODUCTION

Concepts and methods in the social sciences

In general, the behavioral sciences employ a scientific method rather than the chronological method of history. The behavioral sciences are concerned with regular and recurrent behavior; history involves particular and unique events. The prime concepts that the behavioral sciences use are those of culture, society, and personality. It is impossible to study man's behavior without an understanding of all three of these concepts, but different disciplines emphasize different concepts. Anthropology centers on culture, sociology on society, and psychology on personality. In any one discipline, study continually involves all three concepts. Each person must make his own integration of the concepts for the comprehension of human behavior and decide for himself which of them he finds most useful for his own analysis.

The student who makes his own comparison of behavioral science with history finds that the two disciplines contribute different insights. For instance, if he wants to understand why most American families own an automobile, it would help him to know when the car was invented and to acquaint himself with the development of its particular components.

However, he will achieve greater understanding of this behavior if he realizes that our industrial society makes it not only economically possible but socially desirable for families to own cars. In addition to appreciating the necessity for owning cars, he will soon discover what it means for a person to drive a Cadillac rather than a Ford.

Similarly, in order to comprehend differences between northerners and southerners, one must realize that there are cultural and social differences between the regions. Analysis of the two present-day cultures and societies could illuminate much of the antagonism between North and South. However, the contemporary difficulties between the regions could scarcely be appreciated without their historical background. Knowledge of slavery, the Civil War, Reconstruction, and many other historic events is vital for a full comprehension of our regional differences.

Anthropology and the concept of culture

This book introduces one of the behavioral sciences' primary concepts—the concept of culture. This concept has been most fully developed by anthropology and is useful to introduce this field.

Anthropology is most frequently defined as "the science of man." This definition does not tell much about anthropology, nor does it distinguish anthropology from the other disciplines that study man, his actions, and his products. The vague definition does, however, indicate the unusual breadth of subject matter that is characteristic of anthropology; probably no other science attempts to encompass such a variety of areas.

First, anthropology is concerned with both the biological and cultural aspects of man. Man is an animal, similar in some ways to many other members of the animal kingdom. At the same time, he is a human being, possessing culture, which makes him quite unlike any other animal. Anthropologists study both man's physical nature and his culture, particularly the manner in which physical inheritance and culture interact.

Second, anthropology considers man during every period of his history from the time when manlike creatures first walked the earth to the present day. Since written records cover only about 5,000 of the more than 500,000 years of human existence, anthropologists are the sole historians for more than 99 per cent of human history.

Third, anthropology deals with man in every part of the world. Although anthropologists are best noted for studying exotic people, they are equally interested in modern nations. Many anthropologists are now engaged in research problems dealing with our own culture.

Fourth, anthropology examines groups rather than individuals. Neither evolution nor culture can occur in isolation; therefore, the anthropologist studies individuals and their actions only as a means of learning about groups. He is interested in the individual as representative of a group rather than as a unique human being.

Fifth, anthropology takes a holistic view. It does not isolate a specific part of man's body or his culture to study separately. Instead, it attempts to understand human existence as a whole, paying particular attention to the interrelations between man's physical nature and his culture, between culture and environment, and between different aspects of culture.

Although anthropologists are interested in developments in all these areas, the amount of new data and research techniques has become so great that individual anthropologists cannot conduct research in all these subjects. For the purposes of research, anthropology is divided into a number of subdisciplines devoted to different parts of anthropological subject matter.

1. *Physical anthropology* examines the biological basis for behavior. It studies the way in which the human body developed through the processes of evolution and the physical variety that exists among men in the world today.

2. *Archeology* is the study of cultures of the past, particularly those which have left no written records to aid us in understanding them. Anthropological archeology should be distinguished from classical archaeology (note the difference in spelling), another kind of archeology only remotely related to anthropology; classical archaeology is limited to ancient, literate civilizations.

3. Anthropological *linguistics* analyzes the languages of different peoples. Its purpose is to understand how language works, changes, and relates to other aspects of culture.

4. *Social anthropology* and *ethnology* examine and describe the cultures of contemporary people living in small tribes or in branches of a major civilization. Social anthropology differs from ethnology in that the former develops general laws of culture, whereas the latter describes and records the origins of specific cultures.

2

THE BIOLOGICAL NATURE OF MAN

The first section of this book will discuss the biological nature of man, stressing the anatomical similarities between man and other animals and the way in which man's body evolved from earlier forms to produce the diversity of physical types seen in man today. Special attention will be paid to the now extinct forms of man that preceded *Homo sapiens*, the only species of man in the world today. Even in this first part of the book, which emphasizes the physical aspect of human nature, reference must be made to *culture*, the most important single factor that separates man from other animals. Culture not only shapes the mind and character of man but also contributes to the formation of the body that he possesses.

Evolution

The physical characteristics of man arose through evolution, the process by which animals are constantly changing to become better adapted to their environment. When we speak of evolution we must consider millions or even tens of millions of years. Over such long periods, the earth is constantly changing. In the past million years, for example, great glaciers advanced several times into the region which is now the northern

United States, and arctic climates prevailed. As major climactic changes take place, plants and animals living in an area also change; new species of animals, suited to the new environment, gradually appear. Man himself has been affected by the same sort of gradual change.

To understand evolution it is necessary to know something about genetics, the science of heredity. Although genetics is a very complicated subject, everyone understands the basic results of heredity. We know, for example, that the result of mating between cats is kittens, not colts or little fish. We know that children tend to resemble their parents in physical characteristics; we know that stock breeders can produce cattle with certain desirable characteristics by carefully controlling the breeding of animals that already possess those characteristics.

Heredity operates in this fashion because of the nature and action of the cells and the chemical substances of which cells are composed. The nucleus of each of the many cells in the body contains complex structures called *chromosomes*. These structures occur in pairs in all cells except the sex cells. The number of chromosome pairs differs from one kind of animal to another; in human beings there are twenty-three pairs.

Each chromosome is divided into many tiny sections called *genes*, which are causally related to specific physical characteristics and are the actual units of inheritance. Since chromosomes and genes occur in pairs, each individual can have no less than two genes for any given physical characteristic. Actually, very few human characteristics can be shown to be the result of the action of only a single gene pair; most characteristics are influenced by two or more pairs.

Sex cells differ from other cells in that they contain single chromosomes and genes rather than pairs. When the sperm (the male sex cell) unites with the ovum (the female sex cell), the single chromosomes from the two cells come together to produce the normal paired arrangement. An individual thus receives half of his genetic structure from each parent. Since there are many thousands of genes involved in human inheritance, they can combine in an almost infinite number of different ways. Therefore the chance that two individuals could inherit identical genes is infinitesimally small. The only exception is the case of identical twins, who have exactly the same genes because they are the product of a single cell.

Genes provide potential for inheriting physical characteristics but do not determine the characteristics. The appearance of physical characteristics depends on an interplay of potential and environment, the circumstances which affect the development of that potential. For example, an individual may inherit the possibility of becoming very tall but may actually turn out to be short if he suffers from malnutrition or is a victim of some chronic disease.

If all physical characteristics are inherited through genes from parents, how can new and different characteristics appear? New ones appear because chemical changes, called *mutations*, sometimes occur in genes. When a mutation takes place, the change may result in a form that has never existed before, and it may thus provide some totally new characteristic that can be passed on through reproduction.

One must not think that nature purposefully creates mutations to improve animals and men. Mutations occur at random: some bad, some neutral, a few good. Since the bodies of animals are very delicately adjusted mechanisms, most mutations are unfavorable. This is easy to understand when one considers the danger of a slight malfunction in the complex, delicate circulatory and nervous systems. There are, however, some mutations which prove to be useful in particular environments. These mutations can result in evolutionary change because of the process known as natural selection.

The theory of biological evolution was advanced by Charles Darwin in *The Origin of Species*, first published in England in 1859. Darwin presented evidence to show that evolutionary changes had occurred in the forms of animal life and suggested that this was accomplished by a mechanism he termed "natural selection." *Natural selection* means that an animal better suited than others of its kind for life in some particular environment will have a greater chance of surviving and of producing more offspring. For example, deer living in a natural environment that also includes a number of predatory enemies depend for defense upon the ability to detect enemies and to flee rapidly. If a mutation occurs that gives one deer a keener sense of smell or greater speed, this deer will be more likely to survive and to reproduce. Since mutations are inherited, the new qualities will be transmitted to succeeding generations. Over a long period of time, the "improved" variety of deer will increase in number and may eventually replace the original kind of deer. Success in reproduction, then, is the key to natural selection. A characteristic that gives an animal longer life or greater vigor, or that otherwise increases his reproductive efficiency is selected in the struggle for survival; possessors of the characteristic will, on the average, have more descendants than will possessors of other characteristics.

A physical trait gives an adaptive advantage only in terms of a specific environment. A trait or series of traits that may be advantageous in one environment may be disadvantageous in another. In general, highly specialized characteristics adapted to a single limited environment are not beneficial in the long run, for they limit the possibility of successfully meeting changing environmental conditions. Consider, for example, the reptiles of the Mesozoic era. In this era, large reptiles such as dinosaurs were excellently adapted to the warm, humid climates that prevailed over the earth. Toward the end of the era, however, the entire earth began to cool. The adaptations which had suited the reptiles so well in the previous climate became handicaps, and the creatures were unable to adjust to cooler conditions. All the large reptiles thus became extinct, leaving only the few smaller species that are known today.

Evolution, then, proceeds from a basis of new characteristics provided by mutations which, through the process of natural selection, become more common if they represent superior adaptations to the existing environment. When a favorable mutation has occurred in one place, it can spread to other areas through matings of animals outside their immediate group. This spread of genetic material within a species is called gene flow, and the rapidity with which it occurs is a function of factors such as mating patterns and ease of movement. Since the climates of the earth are constantly changing, adaptations to one climate after another lead to the division of animal life into many different kinds. Mutation, climatic change, adaptation, gene flow, and sheer chance have all been contributing factors in producing the variety of animal life that exists today.

There are a few instances in which it has actually been possible to observe evolutionary processes and their results. One such case is melanism (dark coloration) in moths. The moths of Europe have been extensively observed for several centuries; consequently, data exist concerning the different species and the frequencies with which they occur. A century ago, European moths were almost all light in color, although rare dark mutants were known and highly valued by collectors. In the last century, however, the rise of industrialism in cities has created an environment in which darker moths have a distinct advantage. The presence of smoke in the atmosphere near industrial centers results in a darkening of trees and buildings. Light-colored moths stand out very clearly when they rest against these dark backgrounds and are easily spotted by birds and other enemies, whereas darker varieties blend into the background and escape detection. Also, the darker varieties prove to have a superior resistance to the chemicals in the atmosphere. The result of this condition is that in the neighborhood of cities the dark varieties of moths are now by far the most common; in rural areas the lighter varieties predominate as before.

Antibiotic-resistant bacteria provide another example of directly observable natural selection. When a culture of bacteria is treated with an antibiotic, a few individual bacteria usually survive a normal lethal dose. These isolated bacteria, simply by chance, have been favored with a mutation that gives them a greater resistance to the drug. Since the natural competition of other bacteria is removed by the treatment, the resistant strain can quickly grow and multiply. If the quantity of antibiotic is increased, there may again be some survivors, now even more highly resistant. Since the life span of bacteria is short and only a brief time is necessary for the passage of several generations, resistant strains can develop quite rapidly. This phenomenon, which has also been known to occur in hospitals, can cause diseases that are very difficult to cure by methods normally used. Natural selection is thus capable of producing bacteria particularly well suited to survive in a modern world of antibiotics but at the same time has created new problems for medical research.

Fossil remains are a second kind of directly observable evidence of evolution. Fossils are the traces of living things found in rocks and sediments deposited during earlier periods of the earth's history. They usually consist of the bones and teeth of animals, for these are the hardest parts of the body and prove the most resistant to normal processes of decay. These ancient remains show that creatures existed in the past unlike those living in the world today and sometimes directly indicate the stages in the formation of modern animal species. The fossil record for the evolution of the horse documents the development from a tiny creature of 40 million years ago through a series of stages to the horse of today. The existence of fossils related to man that are in some ways clearly more like other primates indicates that evolution has resulted in changes in the form of the human body as well.

Visible indications of evolutionary action are abundant in modern animals. Observation of the variety of animals found in the world today demonstrates instances of physical differences that relate to adaptation to different environments. Man himself is an example of this kind of variation, for there is a clear correlation between the races of man and isolation in different geographical areas. If adaptation to different environments produces changes within a species, it is not difficult to argue that different species or even genera must have arisen in the same fashion. For example, men, apes, and monkeys share so many physical characteristics that it is quite evident, at least to students of evolution, that they must all have arisen from some common ancestor.

Vestigial organs and structures that have no function in modern animals but are presumed to have been of use in ancestral forms are further clues to evolutionary development. These structures in man hint at a relationship to other animals. Although man has no tail, he belongs to a class of animals that does. Inspection of the human backbone shows that the lowest vertebrae are similar in shape to the tail vertebrae of other mammals; in humans these bones have simply been rearranged to curve underneath the pelvis rather than to project externally. Our canine teeth are also silent witnesses to ancestral relationships. Apes and monkeys have large projecting canines that are extremely useful for gouging and tearing, but we have canines that are almost the same size as our other teeth. The roots of human canine teeth, however, are disproportionately large, a vestigial survival from a time when some distant ancestor had canine teeth of a size more appropriate for competition with other members of the animal world.

The study of embryology offers more evidence of evolution. In the process of development from a fertilized egg to a creature ready to be born, many animals develop elements of body structure that are similar to those of evolutionary ancestors. All mammals, including man, pass through a stage of development in which the embryo produces a foundation for gill arches like those of fish. In mammals, this structure soon acquires different uses, but its transitory existence indicates to embryologists that at some point in the very distant past, man had a fishlike ancestor.

The history of evolution

The story of the development of life from its simplest beginnings to the complexity of today is too long and involved to be considered in detail in

TABLE 1.   THE AGES OF THE EARTH

Table 1 provides a summary of the development of animal life. The most important evolutionary events of each era are listed in the right column.

Era	Date (in Millions of Years)	Animal Life
Cenozoic	70–	Age of Mammals; most reptiles die; man appears very late in period
Mesozoic	200–70	Age of Reptiles; first mammals and birds appear
Paleozoic	600–200	Many simple invertebrates; fish appear by middle of era and become important; amphibians appear later; reptiles appear by end of period
Proterozoic	2500–600	Metazoa; fossil sponges; invertebrates appear at end of era
Archean	4500–2500	First life at 3200 million years

this book. A brief summary of evolution in the periods that preceded the development of man must suffice to set the stage for our prime topic of consideration. Some of the most important events in the development of animal life are presented in Table 1, which lists the eras that geologists use in relating the history of the earth.

Also of interest for the student of human evolution is the zoological classification of animals, for this classification is a rough indication of the closeness of biological and evolutionary relationships between animal forms. The animal kingdom can be divided into a hierarchy of groups of successively smaller magnitude ending with the species, the smallest group that does not mate outside itself. The biological classification of man is presented in Table 2. It is assumed that closeness of relationship by classification is an indication of common ancestry. Thus monkeys, apes, and men, all of whom are included in the order called *primates*, are assumed to have originated from a single type of ancestor at some point in the distant past.

The first life, probably of a microscopic form at a level of organization below that of the cell, is thought to have appeared on earth as long as 3

TABLE 2.   THE CLASSIFICATION OF MAN

Table 2 establishes man's zoological pedigree. The left column includes the groupings used in the classification of animal species, and the right column indicates the group at each level in which man is classified.

Kingdom	Animal
Grade	Metazoa
Phylum	Chordata
Subphylum	Vertebrata
Class	Mammalia
Order	Primates
Suborder	Hominoidea
Family	Hominidae
Genus	Homo
Species	Sapiens

billion years ago. From this beginning, a series of slow changes led to more complex levels of organization. During the many millions of years that animal life was confined to lakes and oceans, the development of vertebrates with an internal skeleton and segmented backbone took place, constituting a major evolutionary advance of the Paleozoic era. Fish seem to have been the first vertebrates, but the pattern of organization proved useful in the adaptation of other vertebrate classes to a life on land.

The amphibians were the earliest kind of four-legged land animals. Their adaptation to land was severely restricted, however, by their reproductive system, for they had to return to water to lay eggs. In the development of reptiles from amphibians the link to water was broken by a new system of reproduction based upon the amniote egg, a large, hard-shelled egg that contains membranes and liquids to protect and nourish the developing embryo. Other evolutionary changes in the skeleton and internal organs made the reptiles a much more efficient class for an existence on land than were the amphibians.

The first reptiles appeared toward the end of the Paleozoic era and increased greatly in number and in kind during the succeeding Mesozoic era. The diversification of reptiles is an excellent example of the opportunistic nature of evolution. Once established permanently on land, the reptiles found themselves in an environment that offered many food sources and few competitors. There was a great diversity of available *ecological niches* (potential ways of life) and consequently a selective advantage for many different adaptations. Some reptiles remained small, whereas others, such as the famous dinosaurs, changed into forms of enormous size. Some reptiles became carnivorous and lived by eating other reptiles. There were flying reptiles and some that returned to a life in the seas and lakes. All these changes, of course, took place by the gradual processes of evolution working over the course of long periods of time.

Mammals

Mammals, the class of animals to which man belongs, represent the next step forward in the long path to humanity. Although the development of man himself occurred very recently, other kinds of mammals have existed for a long time. The first developed from reptiles during the Mesozoic era, perhaps as long as from 100 to 200 million years ago. The earliest were few in number and small in size and probably could not compete very well with the many kinds of reptiles. Toward the end of the Mesozoic, however, the environments in most parts of the world seem to have become increasingly unfavorable for reptiles because of changes in land forms, such as the drying of swamps and building of mountains, and because of increasingly colder climatic conditions. Mammals, physically more capable of adaptation to the new environments, began a rapid *adaptive radiation* at the beginning of the Cenozoic era. That is, they increased in number and evolved into many kinds of animals suited to different ways of life. Mammals became so important during the Cenozoic that the era is sometimes called the "Age of Mammals."

In general, mammals are better adapted to life on land than are the members of any other class. Some of the characteristics that differentiate them from the other classes of animals are the following:

1. Reproduction and nurture.
   A. The young develop and are nourished within the body of the mother and are then born alive, in contrast with the egg-laying reproduction of reptiles and birds.
   B. After birth, the young are nourished by the mother by means of mammary (milk-producing) glands.
2. Control of body temperature. Mammals are warm-blooded; they maintain a constant body temperature whatever the external environment. The body temperature is regulated by a very complex system that includes such features as hair or fur to provide warmth, sweat glands to dissipate heat, and a mechanism to increase or decrease the flow of blood to the capillaries near the skin. Heat regulation is closely related to metabolism, and mammals are usually very active creatures. Among other classes of animals, only birds have a heat regulation system and metabolism that allows them to equal mammals in activity and adaptability to cold.
3. Each mammal has a set of teeth that includes several different kinds—some for cutting, some for gouging and tearing, and some for grinding.
4. The respiratory and circulatory systems are better adapted for life on land than are the corresponding systems of reptiles and amphibians, the mammals' chief competitors on land.
5. The brain is larger and more complex, especially in the areas devoted to sensory perception, than is the brain of reptiles or amphibians.

The class Mammalia may be divided into three subclasses: Prototheria, Metatheria, and Eutheria. The first two subclasses are represented by only a few living kinds of animals and are possibly survivals from earlier evolutionary stages.

The only Prototheria alive today are the duckbill (Platypus) and spiny anteater (Echidna), both Australian animals. These animals show reptilian traits in their reproductive system and in a number of minor anatomical features. The female lays eggs but is equipped with mammary glands to nurse the young after the eggs have hatched. Both species of Prototheria have hair but, unlike most mammals, have no teeth. The duckbill has a bill like that of a duck and webbed feet, and the spiny anteater is covered with quills.

The Metatheria (marsupials) are the pouched mammals. Most Metatheria of today live in Australia (for example, kangaroo and wallaby), but a few, such as the opossum, are spread over a larger area. Because the female has a poorly developed placenta, the young develop within the mother's body for only a short time and are born in a premature condition. When they are born, they immediately find their way to a pouch on the mother's abdomen, in which they remain until about one-quarter grown. The pouch has nipples to supply milk for the young. An example of the immature state of the Metatheria at birth is the kangaroo, which is about 6 feet tall when adult but only one inch long at birth.

All other mammals, including man, are Eutheria. The Eutherian female has a placenta, a structure through which nourishment passes from the blood stream of the mother to the blood stream of the foetus. Because of the placenta, the young can be carried in the womb of the mother for a considerable length of time before birth.

Mammalian reproduction is very efficient for survival. The placental system provides excellent protection for the young before birth and permits a long, slow development. The enforced association between the mother and the young gives further safety in post-natal life and makes it possible for some habits of the species to be transmitted by learning.

In the process of adapting by evolution to different ecological niches, the mammals have separated into a number of orders:

1. Carnivora—flesh eating animals such as dogs, cats, and bears.
2. Ungulata—hoofed, herbivorous animals such as cattle, horses, and deer.
3. Primates—the order to which man, apes, and monkeys belong.
4. Some of the mammalian orders have become adapted to environments other than the land. Bats, for example, are flying mammals, and whales and porpoises live in the sea.

Primates

In the classification of mammals, man must be included among the primates. The following are some of the more important physical characteristics that distinguish the primates from other orders of animals:

1. Primates have *prehensile* hands and feet; that is, hands and feet that are capable of grasping objects. To make this possible, the thumb (or great toe) can be turned so that it directly opposes the other four

digits. It might be noted that man has lost the ability to use his feet for grasping, but this is a recent development related to the fact that man stands erect and supports the entire weight of his body upon his feet.

2. The two bones of the forearm can rotate so that the outer bone moves over the inner bone. This makes it possible for the primates to turn the forearm and hand in any direction.

3. The fingers and toes of the primates are equipped with flat nails rather than claws.

4. The clavicle (collar bone) is well developed to provide muscle attachments and support for versatile and vigorous movements of the arms.

5. The snout is less pronounced than that of most other mammals. The reason for this may be primates use their hands for many tasks for which other animals use their teeth. Thus, primates do not need such strongly developed and protruding teeth and jaws.

6. The sense of vision is highly developed. The eyes of most primates are located toward the front of the face and look forward rather than to the sides, as do the eyes of most other mammals. Most primates have *stereoscopic vision*; that is, the eyes focus together and transmit a single image, with depth perception, to the brain.

7. The primates have only two breasts, located high on the chest.

8. Normally, only a single offspring is born at one time.

9. The primates are generalized animals; their physical features are not very specialized for any particular limited way of life. Thus they retain the possibility of surviving in varying environmental situations.

Most primates are *arboreal*; they spend much of their time in trees. Their physical characteristics are well adapted for this way of life, for such features as vigorous and effective use of hands and feet and good vision add to survival chances for tree-dwelling animals. Primates are chiefly vegetarians, but they retain the ability to eat and digest meat. In the wild, some primate groups occasionally vary their diet of leaves, shoots, and fruit by eating insects, birds' eggs, and even small animals. Primates are social animals whose survival depends on group life. The comparison of primate social behavior is so important in understanding human behavior that it will be treated in the section that deals with the origin of human culture.

Zoologists divide the primates into two suborders. The suborder *Prosimii* includes tree shrews, lemurs, and tarsiers, all of which are small tree-dwelling creatures lacking some of the more advanced primate characteristics. Members of this first suborder are far removed from man's present state of physical development and need not be discussed further here.

The suborder *Anthropoidea* includes monkeys, apes, and man. Monkeys are divided into two groups, New World monkeys and Old World monkeys. The New World monkeys, who live in the forested tropical regions of Central and South America, seem to have diverged from the course of human development in the distant past. The lack of any apes native to North or South America suggests that in this hemisphere evolution never progressed beyond the stage of monkeys. The Old World monkeys (Figure 1) inhabit various tropical parts of Asia, Africa, and Oceania. They show a number of characteristics that relate them to man and the apes, although the relationship is clearly a distant one. Apes and men, the other members of the primates, will be discussed in a later section.

There is relatively little fossil evidence of early primates because members of the order have always been rather rare and have inhabited tropical forest environments where the climatic conditions are unfavorable for the preservation of fossils. A general outline of primate history in relation to the subdivisions of the Cenozoic era may be found in Table 3. The fossils available indicate that the first primates appeared during the Paleocene epoch about 60 or 70 million years ago. These earliest primates were small animals resembling members of the modern suborder *Prosimii*. By the Oligocene epoch, 30 million years ago, true monkeys had developed, and in the Miocene epoch, 20 million years ago, the first apes inhabited the earth. Man did not appear until the Pleistocene epoch, not more than 3 million years ago.

The anthropoid apes

In considering the relationship of man to other members of the animal kingdom, we can have little doubt that the group of animals most similar to man in anatomy, size, and habits is the anthropoid ape (family *Pon-*

TABLE 3.   PRIMATE EVOLUTION IN THE CENOZOIC ERA

Table 3 presents the geological subdivision of the Cenozoic era correlated with the history of the primates as indicated by the scanty fossil material available.

Epochs	Dates (in Millions of Years)	Primates
Pleistocene	3–	Development of man
Pliocene	12–3	Ground-dwelling pre-men?
Miocene	26–12	Variety of monkeys and apes
Oligocene	34–26	Monkeys; first apes
Eocene	55–34	First monkeys
Paleocene	70–55	Only Prosimii

FIGURE 1. THE COMMON MACAQUE

The common macaque (Macaca irus) is one of the most widespread of the Old World monkeys, occurring throughout Southeast Asia and Indonesia.

gidae). The close resemblance between man and the apes in basic body structure is evident from simple observation and becomes even more striking when details of the skeleton, musculature, and internal organs are examined. There are, however, a number of physical differences between man and the apes that demand detailed discussion because they are indicative of the separate paths followed by human and pongid evolution.

The anatomical differences that separate man from the anthropoid apes can be summarized under three major headings: posture, brain, and face-teeth. Man is the only primate that walks on two feet. The most common form of locomotion among apes is *brachiation* (swinging between the branches of trees using the hands and arms). This difference in emphasis between the lower and upper extremities as the primary means of locomotion has resulted in a series of anatomical differences between man and the apes. Many of the physical characteristics discussed below are illustrated in Figures 2, 3, 4, and 7.

FIGURE 2. FEET OF APES AND MAN

The feet and partial skeletons are those of (left to right) a chimpanzee, a gorilla, and modern man. The separation of the great toe and the mobility of the foot are much greater in the chimpanzee than in man. The foot of the gorilla is intermediate because his size and terrestrial habits have resulted in an evolutionary modification in the direction of the human foot.

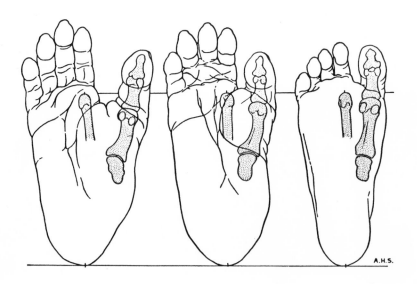

A.H.S.

1. The feet of man have lost the prehensile character typical of primate feet. Man's great toe is in line with the other toes, and all the toes are proportionately much smaller than in other primates.
2. The bones of the back of the foot are enlarged and shifted backward in man to create a heel, which helps to balance the body and serves as a lever to lift the weight of the body in walking.
3. In man, the legs are longer and the arms shorter in relation to body

FIGURE 3. POSTURE OF APE AND MAN

The gorilla (left) is quadrupedal and rarely stands erect. Man (right) and his ancestors have been bipedal for millions of years with resulting changes in the skeleton and musculature.

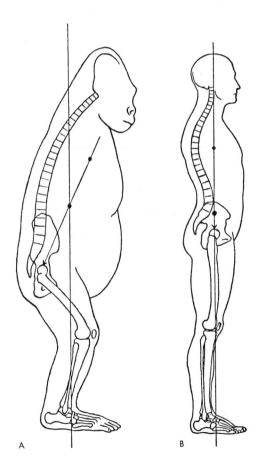

A   B

length than they are in the apes. This, of course, is a direct result of the greater strength demanded of the legs in the human system of locomotion.

4. The human pelvis is short and broad, providing an ample surface for attachment of the heavy muscles necessary to balance man's body in an upright position. The pelvis of apes and other primates is long and narrow.

5. The backbone of man is shaped like the letter S, with a forward curve in the region of the lumbar vertebrae (small of the back) and a second forward curve in the cervical vertebrae of the neck. The backbones of other primates make a nearly continuous forward curve from top to bottom.

6. The rib cage of man is flattened from front to back in comparison with the barrel-shaped rib cage of other primates.

7. The *foramen magnum*, the hole in the skull through which the spinal cord enters, is located directly below the skull in man, whereas in the apes this aperture is more toward the back of the skull. Consequently in man the skull balances on the top of the spinal column and needs only relatively light muscles to hold it in position.

The second set of major differences between man and the apes is in the brain. The brain of man is much larger, averaging 1,350 cc. in modern man as compared to a volume that rarely exceeds 500 cc. in apes. In addition, man's brain is more complex, particularly in the frontal region, where many of his most important intellectual faculties are thought to be located.

Finally, there are a number of differences between man and the ape in the region of the face and the teeth. Both teeth and jaws are much smaller in human beings than in apes, and *prognathism*, the extent to which the jaws protrude beyond the level of the rest of the face, is much less marked in man. Almost the entire skull of the ape is enclosed by heavy muscles necessary to operate the massive jaws, and in some of the larger apes there is a crest of bone along the top of the skull to give additional attachment for the jaw muscles.

Although man and the apes both have the same number and kinds of teeth (2 incisors, 1 canine, 2 premolars, and 3 molars on each side of the upper and lower jaws), there are differences in both the shape of the dental arch and in the shape of the teeth. In primates other than man, the line of teeth has a U shape, with molars and premolars forming almost parallel lines on opposite sides of the jaw and a sharp rounding at the front. In man, the line of teeth forms a parabola, a single continuous curve from the last molar on one side of the jaw to the last molar on the other. The canine teeth in many primates, including all the apes, are sharp, pointed teeth that protrude well beyond the level of the rest of the teeth and serve as useful tools and weapons. In human beings, the canine teeth are much smaller and less pointed and are of about the same length as the rest of the teeth, although the very large roots with which they are still equipped in modern man suggest that these teeth were larger in some of man's ancestors. The first lower premolar teeth in many primates are also large with a single dominant point; in man, all premolars are alike and have two cusps (points) of equal size. In apes and most other primates the molar teeth increase in size from front to back so that the third molar is the largest. In man, the molars decrease in size from front to back.

The human face also presents a number of unique characteristics. Because of an enlarged forehead, reduced jaws, and a chin, man's face presents an almost straight line from top to bottom, whereas the faces of other primates slope backward from chinless, protruding jaws to a receding forehead. Most primates, particularly apes, have large ridges of bone above the eyes, but in modern man these ridges are little developed. The nose of man stands out from his face with a well-developed bridge and extended tip. Noses of other primates are generally flat and broad with little bridge. (See Figure 4.)

The apes of today are rare creatures found only in parts of southeast Asia, the islands of Indonesia, and central Africa. The gibbon and the orangutan are the two existing kinds of Asian apes. The gibbon is the smallest of the anthropoid apes; adults stand about 3 feet tall and weigh from 12 to 15 pounds. The brain averages only about 90 cc., but considering the small size of the body this figure is not proportionately much different from that for other ape species. Gibbons are the most skilled acrobats among the apes and give unrivaled performances of brachiation in their native habitat. They can easily cover 10 feet in a single swing and not uncommonly make leaps of 30 feet when no neighboring branch is available. The movement of the gibbon through the trees is facilitated by an extreme development of the creature's arms, which are about two and one-half times the length of the trunk of the body. It has been estimated that better than 90 per cent of gibbon locomotion is by brachiation. On the relatively rare occasions when gibbons descend to the ground, they walk on all fours but frequently rise to a standing position and run a few steps holding the arms above the head or to the sides for balance. Like all the apes, the gibbon is active during the day and sleeps at night. About 80 per cent of the gibbon diet consists of fruit, with most of the remainder being leaves, buds, and flowers. Birds' eggs, young birds, and insects are sometimes eaten for variety, adding protein to the diet.

The orangutan, which today is found only on the islands of Borneo and Sumatra in Indonesia, is much larger and more powerful than the gibbon. Because its legs are very short, the animal measures only 4 to 5 feet in

FIGURE 4. SKULLS OF APE AND MAN

In the male gorilla (A), the massive jaws dominate the facial skeleton and the small brain case is in back of the plane of the face. In man (B) the greatly enlarged brain case with well developed forehead is directly above the reduced teeth and jaws.

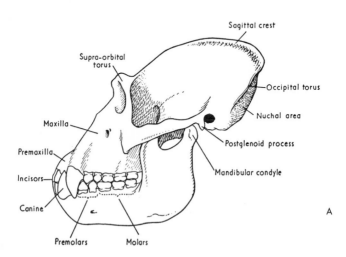

A

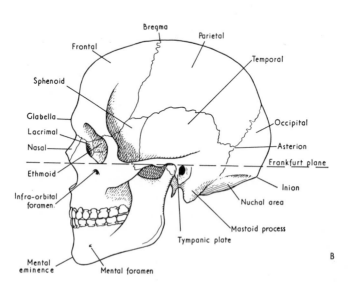

B

height, but adult males weigh between 150 and 200 pounds. There is a marked difference in size between male and female, with females weighing only about half as much as the males. Cranial capacities of adult orangutans range up to 400 cc.

Like the gibbon, the orangutan spends most of its time in trees. Because of its size, however, the orangutan moves slowly and deliberately through the forest, testing branches to see whether they will bear his weight before swinging to them. At night the orangutan descends to lower, larger branches in which he builds a nest.

The two living African apes are the chimpanzee and the gorilla. (See Figures 5 and 6.) The chimpanzee inhabits a wide area of tropical forest in central Africa. Although taller than the orangutan, the chimpanzee is of a much lighter build, the adult male standing about 5 feet tall and weighing about 100 pounds. The legs are longer and the arms shorter than they are in the gibbon and orangutan; of all the apes, the chimpanzee most closely approximates man in limb proportions. Cranial capacities average about 400 cc. Chimpanzees are good brachiators, but they frequently descend to the ground, where they often stand and walk upright. Like the orangutan, the chimpanzee builds a temporary nest in a tree to spend the night. Fruit makes up the bulk of his diet, with occasional vegetable and animal foods.

The gorilla is the rarest of the great apes and occupies only two restricted locations in central Africa. By far the largest and most powerful of the apes, an adult gorilla may stand 6 feet tall and weigh as much as 400 to 500 pounds. Weights of 600 pounds or more have been recorded for adult males in zoos, but this is probably an unusual phenomenon related to captivity. Although the skull of the gorilla is massive, most of it is bone that serves as attachment for the muscles that move the jaws; cranial capacity is only about 500 cc. Gorillas are good climbers and spend considerable time in trees, but their size restricts their activities to the larger branches. When on the ground, gorillas walk on all fours; they are capable of standing upright but find it uncomfortable to do so. In the wild, gorillas eat mostly fruit and vegetables, but in captivity some have grown fond of meat, milk, and eggs.

Little is known about the fossil ancestors of the great apes. The finds that have been made indicate that in the middle of the Cenozoic era (15 to 30 million years ago) apes were more common than they are today, although even then they must have been rare in comparison with other mammals. At this time, apes were found in several parts of the world, such as India and central Europe, where they no longer live, and there were undoubtedly more separate species than there are now. Early apes do not usually show the special adaptations to brachiation, such as the lengthened

FIGURE 5. CHIMPANZEE

The chimpanzee is the most versatile of the living apes, being equally at home in the trees and on the ground. This picture clearly illustrates the prehensile character of the foot.

FIGURE 6. GORILLA

By far the largest of the apes, the gorilla is too heavy to spend much time in trees. On the ground, he walks on all fours planting the feet flat and using the knuckles of the hands for support.

arms that are typical of the gibbon and orangutan, nor do they show the enlargement of teeth and jaws characteristic of the larger apes today.

The pleistocene epoch

Before presenting the fossil evidence that bears directly upon the development of man from a more generalized primate, we should examine the changes that have taken place in the earth in geologically recent times, for these changes provide a useful time scale in studying early man. The evidence of these changes provides both a means of dating early human remains and an understanding of the climatic pressures that may have stimulated the process of human evolution.

We have pointed out that geologists divide the history of the earth into eras, of which only the latest, the Cenozoic era, is of primary interest for this book. Since the 70 million years of the Cenozoic is still a very long time, it is useful to subdivide the era into a number of periods, which have been presented in Table 3. Of these periods, the Pleistocene is of most interest for the present discussion, since it was not until this period that man first appeared on the earth. Just as the Cenozoic era can be called the "Age of Mammals," so the Pleistocene period can be called the "Age of Man."

The Pleistocene was characterized by extreme fluctuations in climate. At least four times during the period, great glaciers covered large parts of the northern hemisphere, extending as far south as the middle of North America and covering the British Isles. In times between glacial advances, the climate became as warm as today's, or warmer. Even areas far from the glaciers were affected, for the climatic changes were worldwide in scope.

One of the effects of the great masses of ice and snow was to change the levels of seas and rivers. The amount of water stored in ice fields can be very large. Even today, the glaciers that cover much of Greenland and Antarctica are in many places more than 10,000 feet deep. It has been estimated that if all this ice were to melt, the level of the oceans would rise 200 feet, enough to cover completely New York City, Los Angeles, London, and many other principal cities of the world. On the other hand, when glaciers were much more extensive than they are now, the seas were correspondingly lower, and many parts of the world that are now under water were dry land: England was connected to Europe; most of the islands of Indonesia were part of the Asian continent; and Alaska and Siberia were connected by a land bridge.

Areas near the glaciers were, of course, very cold, with no trees and little vegetation and only the few species of animals that were equipped to survive arctic conditions. Rainfall was affected all over the world; during the heights of the glacial periods there was considerably more rain in many areas than at present. For example, the Sahara Desert, which today is one of the most arid regions in the world, was covered with dense vegetation. All these changes presented great challenges for both man and animals; challenges that were met by the process of evolution and, for man, by improvements in culture.

To understand the chronology of the subjects that follow, it is necessary to learn the subperiods into which the Pleistocene period is divided. (All these subperiods are listed in Table 4). In all, the Pleistocene is thought to have lasted from 2 to 3 million years, although there is still considerable difference of opinion among geologists over this point.

The first half of the Pleistocene was a long subperiod, called the Villafranchian, during which there were no glaciers of great extent. Instead, the Villafranchian was a time of gradual cooling of the earth following the generally warm Pliocene period, which preceded the Pleistocene. About 500,000 years ago, the first of the great glacial periods, known as "Ice Ages," began. This was followed by a warmer period called the first interglacial period, then by the second glacial period, and so on until the fourth glacial period. At the end of the fourth glacial period, which can be roughly set at 10,000 years ago, the Holocene or recent period began. There is no way of knowing whether the periods of glaciation have run their course or whether we are now merely at the beginning of an interglacial period that will be followed by a fifth glacial period in the far distant future. Evidence from the last century suggests that worldwide climates are becoming warmer, but this trend might be either a minor fluctuation or a pattern of long-term significance.

The australopithecines

If modern man is distinguished from the rest of the primates by his erect posture, large brain, and specializations of teeth and face, the remote ancestors of man must have been more like other primates in these features. Until the last few decades, however, very few fossils had been found that indicated the nature of very early manlike creatures. The first remains of fossil men, such as the original Neanderthal man from Germany, were instructive but too similar to modern man to throw much light on the paths of human evolution. Vital information has been added in the gap separating man from his primate ancestors by a spectacular series of fossil discoveries from South Africa that makes it possible to define a family of primates called the Australopithecines.

The first Australopithecine find, the skull of a juvenile about six years old, was made by Professor Raymond Dart of the University of Witwatersrand in 1925. Although Dart recognized the importance of the tiny skull, most physical anthropologists were reserved in their opinions, for they feared that adults of the species might prove to be much more apelike than the immature specimen suggested. In the 1940's and 1950's, many more Australopithecines were discovered in various parts of South Africa, and the remains of more than one hundred individuals of all ages and both sexes are now available. Dart's original opinion that the Australopithecines are a family of the utmost significance in understanding the course of human evolution has been fully justified.

The most important contribution of the study of the Australopithecines is a knowledge of the different rates of development of the characteristics that mark mankind. It was not known previously whether man's skull, posture, and teeth evolved at the same time and rate, or whether one feature developed first and was followed later by the others. The African fossil finds indicate that posture and teeth had assumed what is essentially a hominid pattern before there was any remarkable change in the capacity of the skull.

The area in which most of the remains definitely identified as *Australopithecus* have been found is the region known as the Transvaal, which lies somewhat inland from the east coast of Africa near the southern tip of the continent. At the time the Australopithecines inhabited the region, the country was open grassland, as it is today, rather than forest. In such terrain, it is not surprising that the Australopithecines proved to be grounddwelling, rather than arboreal, animals. Although experts still disagree about the exact date at which the Australopithecines lived, they must certainly be placed in the early part of the Pleistocene, perhaps at a time equivalent to Late Villafranchian and extending into the early glacial periods. An absolute date determined from rocks associated with one of the Australopithecine fossils was 1.75 million years.

Although there is a great deal of variability among the Australopithecine fossils, it is possible to delineate the general characteristics of the group. The cranial capacity of the finds ranges between 450 cc. and 700 cc., but a few specimens may have had greater capacities. Although the small size of the creatures (usually less than 100 pounds) makes this brain size relatively larger than that of the apes, it is still far from that of modern man. However, in the shape of the forehead and total height of the skull above the ear openings, Australopithecines show a slight advance toward a more human condition. Thus, the areas of the brain dealing with motor control seem to have begun to develop.

All the skeletal evidence that has a bearing on posture indicates that the Australopithecines normally stood upright. The pelvis is remarkably human in general shape (Figure 7), the backbone shows a double curve, the *foramen magnum* is directly underneath the skull, suggesting that the head was balanced for walking erect, and the muscle attachments indicate development of the heavy leg muscles needed for bipedal locomotion.

Australopithecine jaws are large and possess a degree of prognathism that is more apelike than human. The molar teeth are also far larger than those of modern man, but in all other features the dentition follows a human rather than an apelike pattern. The dental arch is a rounded rather than a U-shaped curve, the canine teeth are small and evenly formed rather than pointed, and the premolar teeth, although large, are shaped like those in humans. (See Figure 8.)

There seem to have been at least two kinds of Australopithecines, now usually called *Paranthropus* and *Australopithecus*. *Paranthropus*, the larger of the two, is thought to have been a vegetarian whose way of life led to eventual extinction. *Australopithecus* was more generalized in his diet. He ate both vegetable and animal foods and probably hunted small animals

FIGURE 7. PELVES OF CHIMPANZEE, AUSTRALOPITHECINE AND MAN

The close resemblance between the Australopithecine (B) and modern human (C) pelves and the way in which they contrast with the pelvis of the quadrupedal chimpanzee (A) leave little doubt that the posture of the Australopithecines must have been close to that of man today.

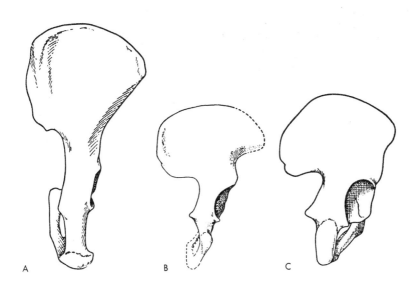

A   B   C

with some regularity. The use of simple tools was advantageous to *Australopithecus*, and physical adaptation to his way of life provided the stimulus for advance to more human forms.

The association of purposefully fashioned tools with an Australopithecine was demonstrated by Dr. and Mrs. Louis S. B. Leakey. Many years of diligent searching of Pleistocene deposits in the Olduvai Gorge of Tanzania, East Africa, resulted in the discovery by the Leakeys in 1959 of an Australopithecine skull in the midst of a collection of crude stone tools and the bones of slain and eaten animals. Unless some more advanced hominid can be demonstrated to have lived in East Africa at this time, the Australopithecines must have been the makers of the tools. Dr. Leakey feels that some of the Olduvai bones from this time or even earlier do belong to an advanced hominid, but most anthropologists do not agree that the existence of such a creature has as yet been substantiated.

It is possible to speculate about the circumstances that gave rise to the Australopithecines. Well before the time at which they lived, there must have been selective pressures that favored the development of a large ground-dwelling primate. The pressures may have resulted from a dry period that reduced the number of available trees and made arboreal life

FIGURE 8. TEETH OF GORILLA, AUSTRALOPITHECINE, AND MAN

The teeth of the Australopithecine (B) are very large in comparison with those of Homo sapiens (C), but the shape of the teeth and dental arch are similar. Most notable is the reduction in size of the canine teeth which are so prominent in the gorilla (A).

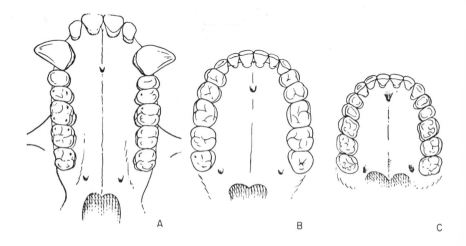

A   B   C

impossible. In fully terrestrial life, defense against predatory carnivores and the ability to secure sufficient food were pressing problems. The use of simple tools such as sticks and stones helped both in defense and in the digging up of edible roots. Any mutation that gave its possessor greater capacity for using tools conferred a decided selective advantage. Therefore, any physical feature favoring an erect posture to facilitate carrying and using tools would tend to be selected, thereby stimulating more efficient tool use and starting the cycle over again. To understand physical development even in the earliest steps toward man, it is necessary to consider the role of cultural propensities.

Other fossil men

The next fossil men to be discussed here are a group named *Pithecanthropus*. Finds of *Pithecanthropus* have been made in two areas of the Far East—the island of Java in Indonesia and the cave of Choukoutien near the city of Peking in China. The Javanese finds were called *Pithecanthropus erectus*, from which the entire group derives its name. The Chinese fossils were first considered to belong to a separate genus and species, *Sinanthropus pekinensis*, but they are now thought to be merely a somewhat different variety of *Pithecanthropus*.

Since little is known about the geology of the Far East, it is difficult to give a very exact date for *Pithecanthropus*. The groups seem to have persisted for a long time, probably from the first interglacial period through the end of the second interglacial period. There is agreement among those who have studied the geology that the fossils from Java are earlier than the Chinese examples.

Although still primitive in many of his physical characteristics, *Pithecanthropus* was considerably more like modern man than *Australopithecus* had been. The size of his brain case is notably larger than that of *Australopithecus*, with the Javanese examples of *Pithecanthropus* averaging about 950 cc. cranial capacity and the Chinese examples, 1,050 cc. The forehead is low and retreating, and the entire skull gives the impression of being flattened from the top downward, with the widest part of the skull at the base, rather than somewhat above the base as in *Homo sapiens*. The bones of the skull are considerably thicker than they are in modern man, and there is a large crest of bone above the eyes. The jaw of *Pithecanthropus* is massive and prognathous and the chin very poorly developed; the teeth, though large, are quite manlike in general form. The limb bones of *Pithecanthropus* are not distinguishable from those of modern man, and the posture was fully erect. Although we would probably find the appearance of *Pithecan-*

thropus startling if we were to meet a living example on the street, we would have little doubt that the creature should be considered human rather than animal.

Since the Javanese *Pithecanthropus* fossils were not associated with tools, we can say nothing about their culture, but there is considerable data about the way of life of the Chinese representatives of the group. The caves at Choukoutien in which the fossils were found were also a living site that gave evidence of the culture of *Pithecanthropus* during the second interglacial period. These caves contained quantities of stone tools made of quartzite. The tools are simple, but the very fact that *Pithecanthropus* was capable of working with such unpromising raw material indicates a fair degree of mechanical ability. Remains of camp fires show that *Pithecanthropus* knew the use of fire, an invention of great importance in providing warmth and protection from dangerous animals that, like man, inhabit caves. Bones of animals that were eaten by the prehistoric inhabitants demonstrate well-developed hunting techniques, for about 70 per cent of them were of deer, an animal that cannot be captured easily with stone tools. There have also been suggestions that *Pithecanthropus* was a cannibal, because a number of the human skulls in the deposit are broken in a fashion suggesting that the brains were purposefully removed, perhaps to be eaten.

Pithecanthropus is now considered representative of a general level of human evolution for which the generic name *Homo erectus* has been adopted. The level is marked by a brain size intermediate between those of Australopithecines and modern man, low skulls with large brow ridges, and several features of dental anatomy not found in man. Fossils thought to be equivalent to *Homo erectus* are also known from Africa and Europe, and assemblages of stone tools from the same time level demonstrate the existence of tool-making beings over most of the tropical and subtropical parts of the Old World.

There is a greatly increased number of fossil finds for the late third interglacial and fourth glacial period. Most of these finds come from Europe and the Near East, which were inhabited by a group of men called Neanderthal. Although the Neanderthals differed from us in many anatomical features, their brain size was as large as ours, indicating that the final major feature of evolutionary development had reached maturity.

Neanderthal men can be divided into two kinds: one, a widespread and generalized type; the other, a specialized type called Classic Neanderthal that centered in southern and western Europe. Classic Neanderthals, who lived during the intensely cold stages of the first part of the fourth glacial period, present a complex of physical characteristics that separates them quite clearly from *Homo sapiens*.

Classic Neanderthal man was characterized by a robustness of the whole body, but particularly of the skull. The skull had an immense bony ridge above the eyes, a relatively low forehead, a flattening of the brain case from the top downward, and a bulging outward of the occiput (back of the skull). In spite of the sloping forehead and flattened skull, the brain case of Neanderthal man was as large as that of modern man, ranging from 1,300 to 1,600 cc. in capacity. The jaws were large and prognathous, and there was no chin. The teeth had several unusual features, among which was a characteristic enlargement of the pulp cavities in the molars. Neanderthal limb bones suggest that a heavy, muscular body accompanied the large skull. Other Neanderthal men show tendencies toward these same features but not the extreme character of Classic Neanderthal.

The fact that the more extreme examples of Neanderthal man were later than examples more closely resembling modern man is now most frequently interpreted to mean that Classic Neanderthal man represents an extreme specialization of evolution rather than a stage in the development of *Homo sapiens*. In the early part of the fourth glacial period, the generalized Neanderthal inhabitants of southern and western Europe were isolated from the rest of mankind and subject to drastic climatic conditions that favored physical change. The peculiar features that mark Classic Neanderthal were simply adaptations to an unusual set of circumstances.

Anthropologists are not agreed about the fate of Classic Neanderthal. Some feel that the group became so extreme that they formed a separate species, which finally became extinct. Others think that those Neanderthals who survived the worst of the glacial conditions reunited with other men as the climate became milder, with the result that the genes were absorbed into a much larger gene pool. Many physical anthropologists now favor classifying Neanderthal man as *Homo sapiens*, implying that the differences between Neanderthal and modern man were minor and would not have prevented interbreeding. Another group of anthropologists, however, thinks that the separate species *Homo neanderthalensis* should be maintained.

The evidence of the culture of Neanderthal man will be discussed later. For the moment we shall say only that Neanderthal man used a series of well-made stone tools, was an accomplished hunter who frequently lived in caves, and had at least a rudimentary religion.

The earliest known remains of anatomically modern man come from European deposits dating from about halfway through the fourth glacial period. These examples of modern man have been given the name Cro-Magnon man, but their skeletons are not distinguishable from those of men living today, and there is no real reason that they should be known by a special name. Although the point of origin of modern man is unknown, his spread throughout the world was relatively rapid.

Suggested Readings

Clark, W. E. Le Gros, *History of the Primates*. London: Order of the Trustees of the British Museum, 1956. Classification and evolution of man and the primates.

Howell, F. Clark, *Early Man*. New York: Time, Inc., 1965. A simple and profusely illustrated account of the evolution of man and his culture.

Hulse, Frederick S., *The Human Species*. New York: Random House, Inc., 1963. A detailed but highly readable text.

Kraus, Bertram S., *The Basis of Human Evolution*. New York: Harper and Row, Publishers, 1964. A good summary of evolution with emphasis on processes.

3

THE HISTORY OF CULTURE

Culture

In studying the biological nature of man, we have treated man as an animal who is physically similar to other animals. The remaining sections of the book will be concerned primarily with another aspect of human existence—the cultural aspect. Since the concept of culture is probably the most important idea in anthropology, it deserves careful consideration. The term "culture" as used by anthropologists has a meaning different from the commonly accepted usage implying skill in certain arts or in the social graces. To the anthropologist, culture includes the beliefs and customs of all men, whether they be educated or uneducated.

Many anthropologists have offered definitions of the term "culture." Perhaps the most frequently quoted is the one proposed by Edward B. Tylor in 1871: "Culture is that complex whole which includes knowledge, belief, art, morals, law, custom, and any other capabilities and habits acquired by man as a member of society." Culture thus includes all the things that we learn from other people; almost all human actions are cultural or directly influenced by culture. Eating is a good example. Food is a necessity of life, and we are stimulated to satisfy the need for food by the natural drive of hunger. The need for food is common to all animals, but in man the satisfaction of the need is closely related to a complex of learned behavior. Members of each culture are conditioned to like some foods and to refuse to eat others, equally nourishing, that they consider disgusting or inedible. How many Americans, for example, would eat worms or grubs even if they were proved to be full of vitamins? The preparation of food is usually carried out in customary fashion unrelated to nutritional values. There are many customs governing how and when people should eat. Man may sometimes postpone satisfying his hunger for cultural reasons, such as religious fasting, or for the simple politeness of not eating in front of others who cannot be invited to share the meal.

What are some of the characteristics of culture? First of all, culture is shared by a group of people. Each person probably has a few idiosyncrasies, things not done by anyone else within the group. These individual habits are not part of culture because they are not shared, but they could become so if they were learned by other people and became customary actions of a group.

Secondly, culture is learned. If a child born in the United States of American parents were moved a short time after birth to some other part of the world, such as India, and brought up by Indian parents, he would develop none of the traits of American culture, nor would he be any more successful than any other Indian in learning American culture at some later time. Among the many sources of learning, the most important is usually parents or family, but playmates, working companions, schools, books, television, and the like are all additional sources. A key to the process of learning culture is the ability of human beings to communicate by means of a language. Although humans, like animals, learn much by simple imitation, many important parts of culture are taught largely by precept. How many children would fail to survive childhood if they had to learn the dangers of automobiles or of poisons by experience rather than by being warned and scolded?

Third, culture is cumulative. Knowledge is stored and passed on from one generation to the next, and new knowledge is constantly being added to the existing fund. Each culture has worked out solutions to the basic problems of life, which it then passes on to its children. The child thereby gains free time to devote to making changes or improvements or facing the new situations he may encounter. The invention of the automobile is a good example of the cumulative quality of culture. The automobile involves the use of wheels and metals, which were invented in the Near East more than 5,000 years ago, rubber developed by Indians in Mexico before the time of Christ, and the internal combution engine from nineteenth-century Europe.

Fourth, culture is diverse. The sum total of human culture is made up of a great many separate cultures, each of which is different from the others. Even in the solution of such a basic problem as providing someone to care for children during the years of infancy and youth, there are a great number of workable alternatives. We must be careful, then, to avoid assuming that our way of doing things is the only "practical" or "right" way. A primary purpose of this book is to illustrate the great diversity of cultural behavior as a means of broadening the reader's viewpoint.

Finally, each culture is a whole, a system with many mutually interdependent parts. For example, the choice of a marriage partner in America provides the beginning of a family, but it also involves many different parts of culture. Religion, economic class, amount of education, and ideas of beauty and romance all play a role. The study of a culture must take the whole into account and cannot explain individual parts until their relationship to the whole has been made clear.

Man is the only animal with a culture, and it is this culture that has enabled him to become pre-eminent in the animal kingdom. To appreciate the importance of culture, consider the possibilities of man's natural animal state. By nature, man is a tropical creature and cannot survive without culture in any cold climate. For defense, he has neither sharp teeth nor claws, nor does he have great speed. He has no natural tools for digging, climbing, or killing to obtain food. Human infants are unable to care for themselves for several years, during which time they prove an additional burden to the mother in seeking to survive.

If man had to live without culture, he would be at a serious disadvantage in comparison to many other animals and would certainly never exist in great numbers. Fortunately, he is not forced to live in this fashion, for by using his well-developed brain he has created culture, which helps him to overcome his physical disadvantages. As a cultural animal, he can provide himself with fire, clothing, and shelter in cold climates. In doing this, he has not sacrificed his ability to live in the hottest of tropical environments. He can invent tools and weapons that serve for defense and aid in securing food. Bipedal habits thus become highly advantageous, for man's hands are free to use the tools he has invented. The length of infancy insures that a child will have an extended training period in which to learn his culture.

Actually, culture is a better means of becoming adapted to an environment than is physical evolution, because it can be acquired far more rapidly. In a few hours or days, man can learn to make a coat or build a fire to warm himself, but to acquire a thick covering of fur by the process of natural selection would take many thousands of years. Culture builds upon culture, and any invention may serve as a stepping-stone to further, and sometimes quite different, inventions. Also, cultural items can be discarded when they no longer serve a useful purpose.

To understand man fully, one must know a great deal about culture. The first cultural topic to be studied in this book is the history of culture from the earliest days of human existence until the present. This vast period of more than a million years is investigated by archeologists, who are the historians of culture.

The work of the archeologist

The goal of archeology is to reconstruct the story of past cultures. If it were possible, the archeologist would write the same kind of account as does the ethnographer who studies a living culture. He would tell how the people lived, what their customs were, what gods they worshiped, how their beliefs and practices changed through time. Many times, particularly when working with very simple or early cultures, the archeologist recovers only a few things upon which to base his conclusions, so he must work like a detective, gaining all possible information from tiny clues and making educated guesses based on what he knows about primitive peoples living in the world today.

To understand the difficulties an archeologist faces, imagine how little would be left of the things around you if they were abandoned for hundreds or thousands of years. Within a few years, all paper, cloth, and flesh would disappear completely; in a few centuries, wooden things would also be gone; in a few thousand years, even bone and metals might disintegrate. Only very hard, imperishable substances such as stone, pottery, glass, and plastics would stand much chance of remaining to be discovered by an archeologist 10,000 years in the future. The things that were left would tell more about some parts of culture than about other parts. They would give a great deal of information about the implements that were used in houses but would tell very little about family organization or about moral beliefs. Since the evidence that the archeologist uncovers may be very fragmentary, it is all the more important that he conduct his investigations carefully and thoroughly in order to abstract all possible information.

In setting out to study a prehistoric culture, the archeologist must first find *sites*, places where people lived and abandoned remains of their culture. From the sites, he can recover *artifacts*, things fashioned by man. Sometimes artifacts are merely collected from the surface of the ground, but more frequently it is necessary to excavate to uncover things that have been buried with the passage of time. The archeologist then classifies and studies the artifacts and compares them with objects discovered by other archeologists. Only after careful and detailed study is he ready to make conclusions about the way of life of prehistoric peoples.

A few examples may help to illustrate the archeologist's use of fragmentary evidence in reconstructing cultures of the past. The form of many tools makes it possible to deduce their function; a knife, for example, must have a sharp cutting edge, and a tool for piercing must be pointed. The number of different kinds of tools left behind by a vanished culture gives information about the way people made a living. Sites that contain large numbers of implements useful for fishing indicate that fish must have been important in the diet, whereas a preponderance of stone hoes among the implements suggests a dependence upon farming. Cultures with large towns and cities may be assumed to have needed some complex form of social control. If, in a large settlement, there are structures of different sizes and shapes, it is usually possible to infer what the functions of different buildings may have been. If a site proves to have a few rich tombs, although the majority of the people were buried in simple graves, it can be inferred that there were class differences within the culture. If the richest burials include war paraphernalia, it is logical to assume that warriors must have been an important part of the upper class. The nature of offerings made to gods, or perhaps images of the gods themselves, can give valuable information about religious beliefs and practices. These examples indicate only a few of the kinds of deductions that are made in archeological research, but they will serve to demonstrate the way in which a great deal of information can be gained about peoples who disappeared from the earth before the dawn of written history.

Two kinds of change are important to the archeologist—changes through time and changes through space. Since we are living in a period of very rapid cultural change, it is easy for us to appreciate the fact that all cultures undergo change as time passes. When an archeologist excavates a site that was occupied for a long period of time, he will find that the culture of the first occupants was unlike that of the last people who lived at the location. In this case, the archeologist may be able to observe *stratigraphy*, a superposition of layers of different ages.

A garbage dump provides an example of the way in which stratigraphy comes about. If a dump began to be used in 1920, the first refuse deposited would contain bottles, tin cans, automobile parts, and other useless or broken implements typical of the things found in homes fifty years ago. With continuous dumping in the same location, a large pile of debris would be built up, deeply burying the earliest material and leaving the most recent on top. A pit dug through the deposit would uncover changes in cultural material. Automobile parts from the upper levels, for example, would be quite different from the 1920 parts at the bottom of the deposit. Other kinds of utensils would show little change. Many of the early hammers and screwdrivers would be the same as those used today. It is this kind of situation that the archeologist seeks to investigate. By taking careful account of stratigraphy, he can build up a long sequence of culture that tells him about changes in the life of the people who lived in an area in prehistoric times.

Culture also differs from one geographic area to another. Clothing, implements, food, and architecture found in a small American town today differ in many respects from those found in a small town in Mexico. On the other hand, there are elements of similarity. One would find that many of the kinds of automobiles used in America are also used in Mexico. In times past, the differences in culture from one region to another were even greater than they are today, for people did not travel so much and there were no large manufacturing centers to supply the same products to immense areas. Archeologists sometimes find that sites only a few miles apart are quite different in culture, although they usually find at least some items that indicate trade or a common style of making things. The differences in culture help the archeologist find the boundaries between people with one way of life and those with another, and the similarities indicate the connections or common traditions that united groups of the past.

The beginnings of culture

At some point in the past, the ancestor of man changed from a culture-less animal to a rudimentary human being with the beginnings of a culture. The very first stages of culture must have been so simple that archeology has not found, and possibly will never find, any evidence concerning them. To reconstruct the way in which culture started, we must imagine the changes that have taken place by comparing very simple cultures of today with nonhuman primate societies. There is no way of proving that conclusions made in this fashion are correct, but general contrasts appear that probably indicate transformations at the beginning of human culture.

The manufacture of tools is one of the prime characteristics that mark human status. It is the manufacture of tools in set patterns, rather than the simple use of tools, that distinguishes man from other animals. A number of animals, particularly the primates, use tools occasionally. Chimpanzees, for example, readily learn to use sticks to reach for things and sometimes throw sticks or stones at an attacker. They may even make tools by altering twigs to shapes appropriate for such jobs as extracting termites from their nests. A tool tradition, however, is unknown in the animal kingdom. When an archeologist speaks of a tool tradition, he means the habit of producing a specific tool in the same manner time after time so that all tools of the same kind look alike. This implies that the manufacturer not only understands the purpose for which he needs the tool but also has in mind an abstract image of the ideal tool for the job. Because stone tools do not disintegrate with the passage of time, they are the best sort of evidence available to archeologists for evaluating the cultural status of man's early ancestors.

There are also very important differences in social behavior between man and the primates, suggesting changes that must have taken place in the development of culture. Primates, including man, are social animals that live in groups. In the organization and function of the social group, however, there are several major differences between apes, or monkeys, and humans. Primate groups are led by one or more dominant animals who must be adult males of proven fighting ability. Among some animals, such as gorillas, there is a single dominant male, whereas among the ground-dwelling Old World monkeys called baboons several older males operate in the position of leadership. Other males are ranked in a set order, each one being able to exert his will over those below him in the social scale. There is also a ranking system among females, but it is less stable than that of the males because periods of sexual receptivity, pregnancy, and lactation tend to change a female's role within the group. Immature animals belong to a series of play groups, membership in which is based upon age. Although dominance is based upon physical force, it promotes peace and order rather than quarrels. Each animal attains his position in the social order while in juvenile play groups and learns to accept it, so that as an adult he rarely challenges a dominant animal to battle.

The social organization of baboons is very evident as the group moves through open country. In the center of the troop is a tight cluster of dominant males, females with infants, and the younger juveniles. Females and older juveniles form an outer rank, and less important males travel at the edge of the troop. If the group is menaced by a predator, the dominant males leave their position at the center and face the enemy while females and infants hurry for shelter in the nearest trees. Cooperation and a division of labor thus characterize baboon defensive arrangements, a system similar to the solution by human groups of the problem of defense.

Organization and cooperation are less apparent in other aspects of non-human primate social life. There is, for example, no family structure or marriage. Ape and monkey females are receptive to sexual attention only during certain periods. At this time, the dominant male has first sexual rights to any female within the group, and other males have secondary rights in accordance to their position in the social hierarchy. Since association between a specific male and female occurs only during the restricted mating period, the ties of longer duration that characterize marriage in human groups do not occur.

Since nonhuman primates have no concept of blood relationship, they lack rules forbidding incest (sexual activity between close relatives). The prohibition of incest, universal among human groups in the world today, must be a custom of great antiquity. This difference in mating habits is related to the size and nature of the breeding groups in human and other primate societies. Among apes and monkeys, all mating takes place within the group, for the presence of animals from other groups is not normally tolerated. In human societies mating within the immediate family is prohibited, and in many simple cultures mates must be sought from outside the entire band of people that live and work together. Reproductively, then, human groups are relatively open, and other primate groups are almost completely closed.

The organization of the group in obtaining food also provides a marked contrast between human and nonhuman primates. For apes and monkeys, getting food is an individual activity in which neither cooperation nor sharing occurs. During feeding, individuals act independently; even the very young obtain their own food as soon as they have been weaned. For human groups, cooperation in the food quest is perhaps the most important function of group life. A division of labor on the basis of sex and age is of the utmost importance in even the simplest cultures known. Cooperation in finding food relates to marriage as well, for husband and wife are typically an economic team in human societies. Male and female engage in different kinds of activities and they, as well as their children, share the results of their labors.

The role of speech in human group life is extremely important, for it is doubtful that the normal kinds of human social control and the degree of cooperation characteristic of mankind could be achieved without at least rudimentary abstract communication. We do not know as yet at what point in the history of human culture the changes in group organization and function took place. It is possible that the Australopithecines may have had tool traditions combined with a social life that was still more like that of the primates than that of man, but there is no way of determining what their social life may have been. When more is known about the control of speech by the brain, it may be possible to say from the shape of the inside of the skulls of fossils whether or not they were capable of speech, but this crucial aspect of human abilities is still little understood.

The paleolithic stage

The most abundant evidence available for the existence and development of the culture of early man is a multitude of stone tools found in many places in Europe, Asia, and Africa. Since each early man must have produced a great many tools during his lifetime, and since stone is more durable than are skeletal remains, we know more about early tools than about the kinds of men that created them. It is possible to outline a general sequence of cultural development covering a period of at least 2 million years. This sequence of development is divided into a number of stages, which are known as the Paleolithic (Old Stone), Mesolithic (Middle Stone), Neolithic (New Stone), Copper, Bronze, and Iron ages in recognition of the materials used for tools in each part of the sequence. It should be noted that the different stages, which are correlated with the subdivisions of the Pleistocene in Table 4, are not of equal length, for the Paleolithic covers far more time than all the rest of the periods put together.

The Paleolithic stage is subdivided into the Lower, Middle, and Upper Paleolithic, with the Lower Paleolithic being the earliest and the Upper Paleolithic the latest. All the cultures that are recorded for the two earliest

TABLE 4. TOOL TRADITIONS AND THE PLEISTOCENE

The pace of cultural change and innovation has accelerated steadily since the beginning of tool traditions. The scale of the Holocene relative to the Pleistocene has been greatly enlarged to accommodate the rapid succession of periods in recent times.

Period	Divisions of Period	Tool Stage	Level of Culture
Holocene		Iron	
		Bronze	Civilization
		Copper	Simple Food
		Neolithic	Producing
		Mesolithic	
	4th glacial	Upper Paleolithic	
	3rd interglacial	Middle Paleolithic	
	3rd glacial		
	2nd interglacial	Lower Paleolithic	Hunting
	2nd glacial		Fishing
	1st interglacial		and
	1st glacial		Gathering
Pleistocene			
	Villafranchian		

subdivisions of the Paleolithic are very simple and are known mostly from stone tools, for little of the other equipment that people may have used has been preserved. Lower and Middle Paleolithic industries (collections of stone tools) are known from only a few places in the world. Tools of this age are scarce, partly because man was still a rare animal and partly because much evidence of these early periods has been destroyed by later glacial action or deeply buried beneath layers of earth accumulated in later times.

The quality of the tools improved slightly from the beginning to the end of this long span of time, but the improvements seem to have occurred very slowly. There are several reasons for this slow rate of progress. One is isolation, for groups of men were so widely separated that there was not much chance for inventions to spread. Another reason is that not much culture had accumulated; the fund of human knowledge was still relatively small. It is also likely that the early men who fashioned these tools were rather uninventive and slow to learn.

The earliest tools that are definitely man-made come from various parts of south and central Africa, where they date from the end of the Villa-franchian, about the same time that the Australopithecines lived. These earliest tools have been called "pebble tools" because they were made from large pebbles of some rock that fractures easily, such as flint or chert. The tools were produced by striking a few flakes from both sides of a pebble, creating a crude pointed implement that could have been used for a variety of jobs, although it probably was not very good for any of them. The pebble tools were succeeded by somewhat more sophisticated "bifaces" or "hand axes," which were also lumps of flint chipped on both sides to form a pointed instrument. By the time of the second glacial period, bifacial tools had spread to both Europe and Asia, but none have ever been found in the New World, which must still have been uninhabited. Other industries of very early origin emphasized the use of the flakes struck off a core rather than the core itself.

People of the Paleolithic period obtained food by taking advantage of the edible plants and animals that nature provided. It is likely that men devoted their time to hunting and fishing while the women and children gathered wild plant foods, insects, and perhaps some small animals. A hunting, fishing, and gathering economy offers a precarious existence, for nature is not very generous in providing natural foods in most parts of the earth. Almost all of each day must be spent in the quest for food, leaving little time to devote to amusement or to intellectual activity. Starvation is always a danger, because in time of want there is no method available to increase the food supply. People must live in small groups and have to be constantly on the move, for the food in any one location is soon exhausted.

Possessions must be few and movable, as the constant wandering in search of food makes it impossible to accumulate more than can be conveniently carried. Since food is so scarce, there is little chance for any individual to become richer than others, although a skillful hunter may be respected and his advice sought in decisions of importance for the group.

By the Middle Paleolithic stage, the time at which the Neanderthals occupied most of Europe, man seems to have become quite efficient at gaining a living by the simple techniques at his disposal. Because the Middle Paleolithic occurred at the time of the intensely cold period at the start of the fourth glaciation, life cannot have been easy, but the presence in Europe of large mammals, such as the mammoth and woolly rhinoceros, provided a rich source of food. To kill the large and dangerous beasts that lived at this time must have required great skill in hunting and the coordinated efforts of groups of men.

There is evidence that men of the Middle Paleolithic had religious beliefs. They buried their dead with care and placed stone tools and food in the graves, suggesting a belief in some sort of life after death. Arrangements of animal bones, in one case a series of bear skulls, were made by Middle Paleolithic men. Could these not be the remains of some cult associated with animal spirits?

This brief summary does not do justice to the painstaking scholarship that has been devoted to the study of Lower and Middle Paleolithic cultures. Experts in Paleolithic archeology have studied artifacts from many sites in great detail and have distinguished a number of different industries, which are designated by such names as Acheulean, Oldowan, and Mousterian. Since the distinctions between these industries depends on minute description of many types of tools, they cannot be considered in a work of this length.

About 50,000 years ago, near the middle of the fourth glacial period, *Homo sapiens* first appeared in southern and western Europe, bringing with him a new set of cultures, which are called Upper Paleolithic. From the beginning, Upper Paleolithic cultures showed inventiveness and diversity in tool types (Figure 9). The techniques of chipping stone reached a point at which the better examples are works of art as well as useful implements. Upper Paleolithic man also learned to produce tools by grinding bone and antler, a technique that does not seem to have been discovered by earlier men. The effectiveness of weapons was increased by the invention of the spear thrower and bow, the first mechanical means of adding to the strength of the human arm in propelling projectiles.

Greater efficiency in cooperative hunting was obtained by such techniques as constructing pitfalls and driving herds of animals over cliffs. Even nature cooperated by providing a climate that, although very cold, favored

FIGURE 9. UPPER PALEOLITHIC TOOLS

These are three of many kinds of stone tools made by Upper Paleolithic peoples. Because these tools were made for tasks that must still be done today, they find their counterparts in a carpenter's tool chest.

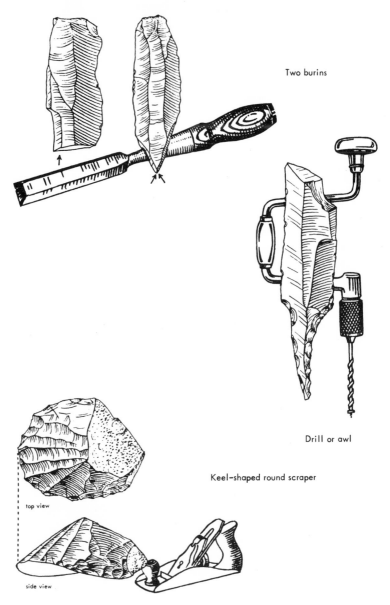

Two burins

Drill or awl

Keel-shaped round scraper

top view

side view

the existence of large herds of animals such as bison, horse, and reindeer. At one site, the bones of 10,000 animals have been found at the bottom of a cliff. Even though these bones must be the result of many seasons of hunting, is seems likely that the communal hunts provided enough food for large gatherings of people. The frequency of Upper Paleolithic sites indicates that the combination of many animals and good hunting techniques permitted an increase in human population.

Upper Paleolithic man sometimes sought refuge from the cold by living in caves, where he could enjoy the warmth and protection of fire. Finds of bone needles and piercing tools suggest that skins of animals, which had earlier been used in unaltered form, were now fashioned to fit the body.

Upper Paleolithic peoples are best known for their art. Drawings of animals on the walls of caves or carvings of men and animals in bone or ivory show such feeling and excellence of workmanship that they have been called examples of the first great school of art in human history. It must be remembered, however, that these representations were more than works of art to their creators; there is strong evidence that they were intended to increase magically the supply of game animals and aid the hunters in capturing them. Many animals are portrayed as pregnant, whereas others are shown as wounded by spears and arrows protruding from their bodies. It is highly probable that these representations are imitative magic by which the artist hoped to bring about events by drawing pictures of them. Some Upper Paleolithic figurines carved from bone represent pregnant women with exaggerated sexual characteristics; again, these can easily be attributed to a cult of fertility. Whatever its purpose, the art of Upper Paleolithic man demonstrates the utmost in technical skill and a genuine appreciation of the forms of nature.

The mesolithic stage

About 15,000 years ago, the great glaciers that had covered Europe began to recede. As they slowly disappeared, widespread changes in climate and in plant and animal life took place. Large parts of Europe changed from open grasslands to dense forests, and the large herds of animals that had fed upon the grass became very rare, their place being taken by forest animals that do not congregate in herds. The Upper Paleolithic cultures, which had been specialized to take advantage of the glacial environment, were no longer adequate. Unlike animals that are specialized for one environment, however, Paleolithic man did not become extinct; he merely changed his culture to a form more suitable to the new surroundings. The new types of cultures of the postglacial forests of Europe are called Mesolithic cultures.

At first glance, the Mesolithic cultures appear to be a step backward when compared to the cultures they succeeded. Most of the fine stonework, the great diversity of tools, and all the beautiful art of the Upper Paleolithic had vanished. Mesolithic cultures were characterized by what are called microliths, very tiny stone blades, many of them smaller than a fingernail. Since the forest animals did not offer such concentrated hunting opportunities, human groups were mostly smaller than those that had gathered for hunting seasons during the Upper Paleolithic, but total population remained quite high. Fishing techniques were developed to a degree not common in the Paleolithic, and man made his first conquest in the animal kingdom by domesticating the dog to aid him in hunting.

An important point about Mesolithic cultures was a willingness to experiment in the solution of problems. Mesolithic people adapted their culture successfully to a number of different environments. The experimentation involved in this adaptation led to the first great revolution in man's culture—the invention of food production.

The neolithic stage

A fundamental change in the relationship of man to nature marked the beginning of the Neolithic stage. This change was so important that V. G. Childe has termed it the "first great revolution" in the history of mankind. The revolution depended upon the development of efficient food production through the domestication of plants and animals. When man ceased to be merely a food collector and began to take an active part in producing his food, he secured the means to overcome the limitations imposed on culture by a gathering economy and entered a pathway that eventually led to civilization.

A given unit of land will produce much more food by being cultivated than by being used for hunting, fishing, and gathering. In most parts of the world, a single family that would need several square miles of land to support itself by a gathering economy can easily produce sufficient food from an acre or two of farm land. When food production techniques became efficient, much more food was available than there had been earlier, resulting in a rapid increase in population. The size of the group that lived together in a single place could also be increased, and for the first time villages of several hundred people became a possibility. With more people living closer together, communication was improved, and contacts between different groups became a matter of everyday occurrence, increasing the speed with which useful inventions could be spread.

The adoption of food production also created a tendency to permanent settlement in a single location. Whereas food gatherers usually have to move frequently, farmers must stay in the same place at least long enough to plant, care for, and harvest a crop. When the need to be constantly on the move was eliminated, it became worthwhile to devote time to building more substantial dwellings and to accumulate large and bulky possessions that are useless to a nomadic people.

Man can increase his food supply by his own efforts. He can put more land under cultivation, obtain more cattle, or improve his methods to achieve a higher yield. This contrasts with the economics of food gathering, in which there is a limit to the degree of efficiency possible. If hunting techniques become too efficient, the wild animals will be exterminated, thus destroying the food supply.

Food production provides more leisure time than food gathering. Although there are periods of the year at which the farmer is extremely busy, there are also many times when the crops need little or no attention. During slack periods, the farmer is free to devote himself to other skills or to amusement.

Finally, by the techniques of food production, a man can produce more food than is actually needed by himself and his family. This possibility of creating a surplus played an important role in the development of civilization, as discussed on pages 53–56.

Several inventions besides the beginning of food production mark the Neolithic stage. The stage takes its name—Neolithic means "New Stone Age"—from the fact that Neolithic man began to prepare stone tools by grinding and polishing in addition to the older technique of percussion. Grinding is a much slower process than percussion for manufacturing tools, and it may be that Paleolithic man was simply too busy looking for food to bother with the grinding technique. With the advent of food production, man had more time for toolmaking, and he found that ground stone tools have several advantages over chipped stone tools. Grinding is an easier process to control than percussion and therefore lends itself to the manufacture of a greater variety of shapes. A ground stone tool can be reground to sharpen the edge when it becomes dull, but a chipped stone tool has to be discarded. Grinding is a better technique for producing the sturdy types of tool that a farmer needs for felling trees and breaking the ground.

Pottery was another invention of the Neolithic stage. The Neolithic people needed vessels for cooking and storing their food. Since pottery is easily broken, it is not practical for a nomadic people, but it is very useful for settled villagers. Pottery was also a marvelous invention from the point of view of the archeologist, since it was used and broken in great quantities, lent itself to rapid changes in style and decoration, and is so indestructible that fragments are almost always preserved for discovery by archeologists.

The manufacture of textiles also began in the Neolithic period. The weaving of plant or animal fibers into cloth provided clothing and other articles that were lighter in weight and more easily decorated than was the skin clothing of earlier peoples.

It is interesting to note that three of the inventions just mentioned—agriculture, pottery, and textiles—were probably made by women. Each of these crafts is traditionally associated with women among primitive peoples and, in spite of notions of male superiority, it is difficult to imagine that prehistoric males would have stooped to the experimentation necessary to make these advances possible.

The basic unit of the Neolithic peoples was the village, a small settlement of a few hundred people. Most Neolithic cultures subsisted by means of a mixed economy, including both farming and animal husbandry, but of these two food sources the planting of crops was most important. There were only a few cultures in which domestic animals furnished the sole or primary means of subsistence. Each Neolithic village was independent and could be self-sufficient in times of emergency, but trade with neighboring villages and even with distant regions was common. Items from known sources, such as seashells, precious stones, and various special kinds of rock for tools, are not infrequently found hundreds or even thousands of miles from their place of origin, so we must assume that Neolithic peoples took a lively interest in trading both practical and decorative items. Land in Neolithic times was probably considered the communal property of the village, and the most important social groupings were based on kinship.

Where and how did the epic invention of food production take place? Strangely enough, it did not occur in any of the areas that today are the centers of world civilization, but rather in the Near East, in an area now underpopulated and underdeveloped. The wild grasses ancestral to the grain crops, the basis of Western civilization, are found in the Near East. Here too are the wild ancestors of modern domestic animals such as sheep, goats, and cattle. During the Mesolithic stage, this area was occupied by a number of food-collecting cultures, the best known example of which is a culture of about 8000 B.C. called the Natufian. The Natufians were still nomadic hunters and gatherers who lived in caves during bad weather and probably had open camp sites at other times of the year. There is nothing rich or unusual about Natufian culture, but the remains of sickles made of microlithic flints hafted in bone or stone show that the people gathered the grainlike grasses of the area and may even have begun intentional planting.

At some point in the Mesolithic, an inventive person must have noticed that seeds dropped near the living sites took root and sent up new stalks. He (or probably she) decided that it would be possible to plant seed intentionally in some convenient location to save the trouble of looking for the plants. With this simple act, agriculture began.

Why was such a seemingly obvious idea so slow to appear? Part of the answer is probably that the earliest cultivated plants provided very little food. One can imagine the first agriculturalist being ridiculed by her companions for wasting time in such an unproductive enterprise. Agriculture could not become important until more productive plant varieties were developed by hybridization, mutation, and careful selection of seed of the best quality.

The development necessary to make domestic plants and animals an effective means of subsistence took place in a part of the Near East called the Fertile Crescent. This region is a crescent-shaped strip of land, the southern end of which lies in the valley of the Nile River in Egypt. From Egypt the Fertile Crescent extends northward along the Mediterranean coast of Palestine and Syria and then swings inland through the ancient land of Mesopotamia in the valley of the Tigris and Euphrates rivers in modern Iraq and Iran. Most of the area is very dry with almost no rainfall, but the water of springs and the great rivers makes highly productive agriculture possible.

Archeologists used to believe that the domestication of plants and animals took place in the river valleys. They argued that at the time food production began, the river valleys, which had had abundant rainfall during the glacial period, were gradually becoming arid, forcing plants, animals, and human beings to congregate at springs and along river banks where water was still available. The close association necessary at water sources was supposed to have provided man with the opportunity to observe and domesticate both plants and animals.

This theory, however, is no longer considered correct, for scientific investigations in recent years have provided two major objections. First of all, geological evidence suggests that the dessication of the Near East took place long before the invention of food production. Second, archeological research indicates that the earliest farming villages were not close to the rivers but were in the foothills that form the margins of the Tigris-Euphrates valley. The foothill region receives somewhat more rain than do the valleys, and the moisture is sufficient to produce a single crop of grain each year without an artificial supply of water. The ancestors of the grain crops are also foothill, rather than valley, plants.

A typical early farming village in the foothills of the Fertile Crescent was excavated by Professor Robert Braidwood of the Oriental Institute of the University of Chicago. The site is called Jarmo and is located north of the Tigris River in Iraq. Around 7000 B.C., Jarmo was occupied for several hundred years, during which time the village was rebuilt several times, leaving a mound of earth and debris 15 feet in height.

Excavations revealed that the people of Jarmo grew wheat and barley that they stored in bins in the floors of their houses. They raised cattle, sheep, and goats and added to the meat supply by killing a few wild animals. The houses were small structures with mud walls, of a size suggesting that each was probably occupied by a single family. There were no large houses, public buildings, or temples, so the inhabitants must all have been simple farmers with no complex form of government or of religion. The population of Jarmo is estimated at about 150 people. Tools from the site were mostly of types that would have been useful in agriculture: hoes, grinding stones, stone bowls, and so on. Metal was unknown. Real pottery appeared only in the upper levels at Jarmo, but in the lower levels there were small pits in the floor, lined with baked clay, that may have been the forerunners of pottery.

Jarmo dates from about 7000 B.C. It seems likely that the techniques of food production became efficient enough in the foothills of the Fertile Crescent to permit permanent farming villages at some time between 8000 and 7000 B.C. Shortly thereafter, when farming spread to the river valleys, villages sprang up rapidly along the banks and around permanent springs in the arid lowlands. Agricultural villages also began to appear in Egypt, where they took advantage of the land that was inundated each year by the spring floods of the Nile.

After agriculture and animal husbandry had reached full efficiency in the Near East, the techniques spread slowly into Europe by two routes, one along the coasts of the Mediterranean and Atlantic, the other up the Danube River basin into the heart of Europe. The spread was so gradual that the northern parts of Europe did not reach the Neolithic stage until 2000 B.C., long after the Near East had advanced to civilization.

The invention of agriculture took place independently in the New World. Evidence for the development of agriculture in the Americas is particularly complete because of recent excavations by Dr. Richard S. MacNeish in the Tehuacan Valley in central Mexico. Refuse deposits recovered from caves in this valley were so dry that delicate plant remains had been preserved for thousands of years, giving an actual record of the diet of the prehistoric inhabitants. The evidence shows that the inhabitants began to plant a few crops long before they took up a fully settled village life. There are remains of domestic squash, beans, and avocados from levels dated at 5000 B.C. Domestic corn appeared at 3400 B.C.

The early corn from Tehuacan solves a mystery that has puzzled biologists for many years. Corn is one of the world's most important food crops, but no one has ever found a living wild plant from which domestic corn could logically be descended. The Tehuacan collections contain fragments of a wild corn with tiny ears no more than an inch long. Each of the kernels was enclosed in a tiny husk and had a hard covering like the popcorn of today. When this insignificant plant was domesticated, it went through a series of modifications aided by hybridization with other plants and eventually attained greater size and productivity. Domestic corn seems to have provided such stern competition for its wild cousin that the latter became extinct.

The first permanent settlement did not appear in the Tehuacan Valley until 3400 B.C., and even then only about 30 per cent of the diet came from domestic plants. The first attempts at food production, then, clearly did not lead to rapid cultural advance. For more than 2,000 years food production was only a secondary source of subsistence in a culture that differed little in settlement and social organization from the cultures of other food gatherers. It is quite possible that an equally lengthy period of incipient cultivation occurred in the Near East as well, but no conclusion will be possible until some early site yields plant remains as well preserved as those of the Tehuacan Valley.

Civilization

The first human revolution, the beginning of food production, contained within it the seeds of a second revolution, the appearance of civilization. Civilization, like food production, began in the Fertile Crescent. Between 6000 and 3000 B.C., a series of inventions and changes transformed the Neolithic cultures of the area into the first civilization. Economic and technical progress provided a necessary base for the transformation, but of even greater importance were social changes that elevated culture to a level of complexity that had never before been possible.

The key to the new way of life was the production of a dependable surplus of food. This surplus not only made possible a marked increase in population but also provided the wealth and leisure time necessary for the development of new forms of social organization. When one man can produce enough food to feed several families, a reorganization of society can take place. Some men can be completely freed from the food quest to specialize in producing goods or supplying services, thus opening the way for skills that demand long training and continuous practice.

Surplus also makes possible the development of urban life. Enough food can be obtained by concentrating the surplus food from productive farming areas to feed city dwellers, who are not themselves food producers. Urban life fosters an increased complexity in economic and political systems, for there must be trustworthy mechanisms to ensure that food reaches the inhabitants of the city and a means of securing the cooperation of the food-producing portion of the population. The procurement of raw materials for manufacturing, the exchange of manufactured items for food, the transportation of commodities, and many other parts of a complex economic system create an interdependence among large groups of people. The self-sufficiency of the Neolithic community must be sacrificed in urban society.

Large-scale public enterprises, such as the construction of irrigation systems, temples, or civic buildings, depend upon the joint effort of many workers supervised and controlled by social or political agencies. Administration and control are related to a concentration of goods and power and the rise of social distinctions between rich and poor or between rulers and ruled.

Improved communications link wide areas to create an atmosphere in which knowledge and inventions spread rapidly. The inevitable conflicts that arise between different units of a civilization or between civilized people and barbarians also play a role in progress, for they make defensive inventions necessary and provide a means by which elements can move quickly from one culture to another.

A simple Neolithic village and a city represent very different kinds of social entities. A Neolithic village is independent and self-sufficient and has less extensive contacts with outsiders. All the villagers are of the same rank and occupation. There are no complex economic, religious, or political systems. A city, on the other hand, is dependent upon large and complex systems; it devotes much time to enterprises unrelated to the production of food but dependent upon food surplus; it includes people of different social classes and different occupations; and the inhabitants are interdependent in a manner based upon strong social control.

Of course, the social changes mentioned here were intimately related to technological improvements and inventions. The invention of metallurgy and the wheel, the use of animal power in plowing and in transportation and of the wind for propelling sailboats, and the development of architecture in brick and stone were all factors that increased the efficiency of human effort or gave room for the expression of a taste for luxury or grandeur. There was a marked increase in scientific knowledge and achievements. Metallurgy, architecture, and the design of wheeled vehicles all require a body of knowledge controlled by specialists. Similarly, writing and astronomy were learned skills made necessary by the increasing complexity of culture. Without these inventions, the civilization of the Fertile Crescent would have been much slower in developing or might never have arisen. At the same time, the changes in social life provided a concentration of ideas without which the inventions might have been impossible.

The geography of the Fertile Crescent is particularly appropriate for the formation of complex societies and city life. The heart of the area—the valleys of the Nile River in Egypt and the Tigris-Euphrates rivers in Mesopotamia—is a region in which life is totally dependent upon the utilization of water from the great rivers. Rainfall is so scanty that crops will not grow in locations that are not watered, either naturally or artificially. Furthermore, the streams provide only a small amount of arable land until they are harnassed by man to suit his needs. At the mouths of both the Nile and Tigris-Euphrates, the rivers in a natural state create huge swamps that are too wet to serve for agriculture. Only when complex drainage systems create set channels can any appreciable amount of cultivable land be obtained. Upstream, the rivers alternate between low water, at which only the banks receive moisture, and high water, when dangerous floods menace crops and settlements. Here too the flow has to be controlled by man, and irrigation channels are needed to supply water during times when the level is low.

The effort necessary to utilize the water of the rivers effectively is too large to be attempted by individuals or by small families. Progress depends upon large groups of men working together to secure mutual benefits. The profits from such large-scale cooperation justify the effort, for the land of the river valleys is exceedingly fertile and can be farmed year round when water is available. Once water-control projects are underway, they not only encourage cooperation by their success but can also provide a highly effective method of coercion, for a recalcitrant farmer can be deprived of water for his fields.

Fruit trees such as the fig, date, and olive are native to the river valleys and provide an additional and welcome new source of food. Tree crops serve as a stimulus for permanency of land tenure in that they take a long time to mature but continue to bear fruit for many years after they reach maturity. The geography of the Fertile Crescent also fosters trade and contact between peoples of different regions, because the river valleys are totally lacking in such important resources as stone and metal ores. The trading of the rich agricultural products of the valleys for raw materials from regions where agriculture was not so successful helped civilization to diffuse outward to marginal areas.

More than half a century of intensive archeological research in Mesopotamia has produced data that illustrate the actual development of civilization in that area. By 5000 B.C., Neolithic farming villages were well established throughout the region, and we may assume that the technical efficiency of agriculture had improved considerably since its hesitant beginnings. About 4200 B.C., a farming people called the Ubaid people moved into the swampy delta of the Tigris-Euphrates and began the task of taming the river. Many of the sites established at this time continued to be occupied for several thousand years, becoming such historic sites as Kish, Lagash, Erech, and Eridu. Archeological excavations in the deepest levels of these sites reveal simple Ubaid villages, at least one of which was so deprived of dry land that its earliest level was built upon a platform of reeds laid on the alluvial mud.

From the first, the efforts of the Ubaid settlers seem to have been well rewarded, for there is evidence of a steady increase in social complexity. In the construction of houses, for example, a differentiation in building materials soon appeared. Most of the people lived in simple reed huts, but some of the larger houses were made of a new material, sun-dried mud bricks. Because of the greater size of these brick houses and the greater effort represented by their construction, it is likely that a class of chiefs or wealthy people was beginning to form.

The surplus of the community was also devoted to creating a worthy place of worship for the gods. At the site of Eridu the lowest levels, which dated from the Ubaid period, revealed a very simple temple, little larger than a house. As time passed, the Eridu temple was rebuilt several times, always on a larger and more luxurious scale. Gradually, the temple complex took on the form of the typical Near Eastern *ziggurat*, a temple placed upon an artificial mound that raised the god closer to heaven and elevated his worship above the heads of the common people. The worship of the gods must have been increasingly controlled by a class of priestly specialists who conducted the rites and administered the wealth necessary for temple maintenance. The Ubaid people seem to have known how to cast metal, but metal was still very rare and used mostly for ornaments rather than for tools. They may also have invented boats with sails; the earliest pictures showing sails come from Ubaid sites.

The Ubaid period was followed by a period called the Protoliterate, during which the final inventions and achievements of early civilization became a part of the culture of the area. Although there is some uncertainty about the exact date for the beginning of the Protoliterate, 3700 B.C. may be accepted as accurate within a century or two. Technological advance continued during this period, adding several major inventions to the cultural inventory. The wheel came into use, first for pottery and, by 3500 B.C., for wheeled vehicles as well. Animal power was adapted to agricultural purposes, making large-scale plowing possible. By 3500 B.C., the first steps toward a system of writing had taken place. The increasing complexity of society must have made it extremely difficult to remember all the transactions and obligations, so man invented a system of notation for keeping records. The first inscriptions were pictographic, using actual drawings of the things represented along with a simple system of numerical representation. Later, these realistic symbols became abbreviated in form and eventually changed to the abstract conventional signs that are the basis of true writing.

By 3000 B.C., the time at which true history is considered to have begun in Mesopotamia, the structure of society had been transformed from Neolithic simplicity to the complexity of civilization. Instead of the village, the basic unit was the city-state, a small but urban center with subsidiary villages and rural farming areas under its control and protection. The system of government was theocratic—a complete fusion of church and state. No division existed between civil and religious authority; the hierarchy of priests also acted as civil authorities. Wealth was concentrated in the hands of a limited class of priests who were believed to hold it in trust and to administer it for the chief god of the city, who was the focus of authority. The god's temple was, of course, the most imposing structure in the city. It not only served as the religious center but also housed a priestly corporation that was the principal landowner and the heart of the economic and industrial systems of the city. The staff of the temple included a great number of priests of various ranks, as well as administrators, workers, and slaves who took care of the worldly possessions of the god. Craft industries and trade were probably both monopolies of the temple corporation in these early times. Only the temple had the capital to finance them and the need for the articles they produced.

Although there are ample documents to show that struggles for power between the city-states were frequent in early Mesopotamia, a true empire covering a large territory seems never to have been established before the reign of Sargon of Akkad around 2300 B.C. By the time of Sargon, secular authority in the hands of a king backed by military power had usurped the dominant role held by the temple in earlier times. This social transformation and the rise and fall of empires that followed Sargon are matters of history and cannot be pursued further in this book.

Mesopotamia, of course, is only one example of early civilization. The Egyptians kept pace with the development of Mesopotamian civilization, organizing a society that permitted the construction of the great pyramids by 2600 B.C. A still little known civilization occupied the valley of the Indus River in northwestern India, leaving the great ruined cities of Harappa and Mohenjo-daro. In the Orient, civilization developed first in China, then in Japan and Southeast Asia. The American Indians followed an independent pathway to civilization. In the first five hundred years of the Christian era, native American civilizations arose in Mexico and Central America and in Peru.

Suggested Readings

Braidwood, Robert J., *Prehistoric Men*. Chicago: University of Chicago Press, 1957. A brief account of culture history.

Childe, V. Gordon, *What Happened in History*. New York: Penguin Books, Inc., 1946. A classic summary of the stages of cultural development.

Daniel, Glyn E., *The Idea of Prehistory*. Cleveland: The World Publishing Company, 1963. The development of the science of archeology.

Editors of *Life*, *The Epic of Man*. New York: Time, Inc., 1961. A fully illustrated history of man's culture.

Hole, Frank, and Robert F. Heizer, *An Introduction to Prehistoric Archeology*. New York: Holt, Rinehart and Winston, 1965. A consideration of the aims and methods of archeology.

Redfield, Robert L., *The Primitive World and Its Transformation*. Ithaca: Cornell University Press, 1953. A consideration of the impact of civilization on man's way of life.

4

THE PHYSICAL CHARACTERISTICS
OF MODERN MAN

The preceding chapters of this book have been historical; they have traced the gradual development of man's physical and cultural aspects. Anthropology, however, is not only a science of past events: it also studies man as he exists today. The discussion of evolution and fossil man has retraced the pathway to *Homo sapiens* but has not considered the diversity that exists within our species today. Actually, modern diversity is nothing more than the result of the same processes that formed *Homo sapiens*.

Modern physical anthropology

The science of physical anthropology has undergone a radical change in emphasis in the last fifteen years. Before this change, physical anthropologists were primarily concerned with simply measuring and describing the physical characteristics of modern and fossil men. Training and research in physical anthropology were devoted to performing and recording accurately large series of measurements and observations of physical traits, particularly those traits associated with skeletal structure. One physical anthropologist, for example, is said to have made more than five thousand measurements on each skull he studied. Such diligent collecting of data must be understood as necessary in the early stages of any science, for not until many facts are known can serious attempts at explanation and interpretation be attempted. The measurements had practical applications as well; a knowledge of the form and variation of the human body is useful in such diverse projects as the design of furniture and space capsules, the planning of the production of factory-made clothing, and the identification of human remains for the police or for war casualty files.

Some physical anthropologists, however, went to the extreme of acting as though measurements were an end in themselves. They seemed to believe that by increasing the number and accuracy of measurements and by classifying and comparing men on this basis, they would ultimately arrive at solutions to all possible problems in physical anthropology. The chief objection to this philosophy is that measurements have little meaning unless they are based upon a thorough understanding of the operation of the human body and of the mechanisms by which physical change occurs.

A concrete example may help to clarify the need for functional understanding. Measurement of the human ilium—the hip bone—shows that the total length of the bone is the same in males and females. To conclude from this fact that the bone is alike in males and females, however, is quite wrong, for an understanding of the function of the ilium in the living body indicates a marked sexual difference. The ilium consists of two parts, an upper section that serves as an area for muscle attachment and articulation to the backbone and a lower section that is an important part of the pelvic inlet. Since males are usually larger and more muscular than females, the upper part of the bone is long in males and short in females. The lower section, on the other hand, is short in males and long in females, who need a large pelvic arch to facilitate childbirth. Understanding what the ilium serves for in the human body leads directly to a series of measurements illustrating sexual differences, whereas a failure to consider function might easily result in misinterpretation.

In attempting to understand function and process, the new approach to physical anthropology has become broader and more closely related to the other natural sciences. The modern physical anthropologist must study both human and animal anatomy to be equipped to consider bones as parts of the body that are designed to serve some role in a living creature. He must be versed in genetics so that he can interpret the manner in which evolutionary changes in the human body may have taken place. Some physical anthropologists now study the growth and development of children. Others are concerned with somatology, the study of the general form of the human body and the relationships that may exist between body form and temperament or health problems. It should be pointed out, however, that somatology is still a highly controversial subject, for many anthropologists feel that body form is too influenced by environment to be of any determinable genetic significance.

The underlying philosophy of the new physical anthropology is that evolution is the prime causative factor in human variability. Since evolution is a very complex process, one cannot expect simple solutions to all problems but must slowly build basic knowledge by careful study, experiment, and a better knowledge of human genetics. Although still in its infancy, the new physical anthropology has made a contribution by criticizing the sometimes sterile methods of the old school, which failed to recognize the complexity of physical variability.

The races of mankind

The foregoing discussion of the philosophy of modern physical anthropology should make it evident that the science does not hope to provide simple answers to questions about the nature of races, the characteristics that distinguish one race from another, or the direction that the diversification of mankind may take in the future. One of the chief purposes of the following discussion of physical variation among modern men is to indicate the complexity of the subject and the futility of seeking understanding through dogmatic generalizations.

In regard to race, as to other topics, the thinking of physical anthropologists of today differs greatly from that in vogue a generation ago. In earlier times, races were thought of as quite separate, immutable entities that were little affected by the processes of evolution. Today, the emphasis rests upon the fact that man is a single species showing gradual variation between extremes because of the action of evolutionary change.

The homogeneity of modern man should be emphasized before the discussion turns to the question of variability. All living men belong to a single species. Considering the tremendous extent of territory and the variety of environments covered by mankind, the degree of physical differentiation is surprisingly low. Other animal species covering as wide a territory often separate into a number of quite distinct species. The prime factors in maintaining the unity of mankind are probably the use of cultural rather than physical adaptations to environment and a high degree of mobility.

Animal species show the characteristic of variability—physical differences between individuals and between groups. Any observer of mankind can easily note that men from one part of the world differ in some characteristics from men of other regions. If, for example, one were transported directly from northern Europe to central Africa to eastern Asia, one would see that the inhabitants of each location are different from those in the others. If a sample of one hundred individuals from each of these locations were to be brought together and thoroughly mixed, it would not be difficult to sort them out again into the original groups, although there might be a few individuals whose assignment would be in doubt.

Imagine a second journey, extending from northern to central Europe to southern Europe, again collecting a sample of one hundred individuals from each of the three locations. An observer would note some physical differences between the inhabitants of the three areas; but the differences would be considerably less than in the former case, and the sorting of individuals from a mixed sample would include many more doubtful choices. If the distance were decreased to include three villages only 50 miles apart, it would probably be impossible to note any systematic physical differences between groups from the three locations.

Physical differences between groups of men thus increase with increasing distance between the groups. Differences also tend to become more marked where there are barriers that impede communication. A distance of 500 miles might be associated with little physical variation along the valley of a large river that served as a natural route of travel but be associated with considerably greater variation where the distance spanned a barrier such as a great desert or major body of water. These facts are in accord with the general principle of evolution that groups of a single species that are separated from one another tend to develop differences in physical features.

Another feature of variability is that there are not only differences between groups but also differences within groups. Nobody would expect to find a group the members of which were so alike that they could not tell each other apart. The differences within the group may be expected to be smaller than those that separate the group from other groups, but they still exist and have existed since the beginning of mankind.

Modern physical anthropology insists that the study of physical variation among *Homo sapiens* should deal with groups of people living in proximity, which are termed *populations*, and should compare populations in terms of the *frequencies* with which characteristics occur in the group. A population is a group of people within which genes are freely exchanged by mating; that is, there are no physical or social barriers to breeding. An anthropologist can observe and measure a population and record the frequency with which various characteristics occur. He can then compare these figures with the frequency figures for other populations and state the differences that exist.

As an example, an anthropologist might observe a population in northern Europe to consist of 30 per cent blond people, 50 per cent people with light brown hair, 16 per cent people with dark brown hair, and 4 per cent people with black hair. In so doing, he is describing an actual situation and dealing with people as he finds them. Anthropologists in the past frequently used figures of this sort to jump to the conclusion that at some time in antiquity northern Europe was inhabited by a group of people all of whom had blond or light brown hair. They then attributed the genes for darker hair found in northern Europe today to migration of people into the area from somewhere to the south, even though there was not the slightest bit of evidence for such migration. Once speculation of this sort, which is not based upon historical evidence, is accepted as valid, there is no end to the extremes to which it can be carried. One racial classification explained the inhabitants of India as a composite race made up of a mixture of Mediterranean Caucasoid + Australoid (natives of Australia) + Negrito (pygmy Negroid peoples) + minor fractions of Iranian Caucasoid, Nordic Caucasoid, and Mongoloid. It is not impossible that such a mixing could have taken place in the past, but there is no archeological evidence whatever that would substantiate it.

In order to recognize the diversity that exists within *Homo sapiens*, one can divide the species into major groups that correspond well with the principal land masses of the world. These major groups are called "stocks" by some anthropologists and are called "races" by other anthropologists and in general usage. The five major divisions of mankind most commonly recognized are the following: Negroid, the people of Africa south of the Sahara Desert; Caucasoid, the people of Europe; Mongoloid, the people of eastern Asia; Australoid, the aborigines of Australia; and the American Indian, the native inhabitants of North and South America. The territories in which these five groups reside are relatively isolated from each other by physical barriers, but even these barriers do not prevent the existence of marginal populations that are intermediate between races in their physical characteristics. It should be noted that this system of classification leaves out the inhabitants of several areas of the world, such as those of India and the Pacific islands of Oceania. Both of these regions are areas of considerable physical diversity. They are difficult to classify under any scheme and are probably best handled by being separated into a number of populations.

It is possible to subdivide further the inhabitants of each of the major areas. The people of Europe have frequently been divided into four or more smaller groups which are called "races" or "subraces," depending upon what term is used for the larger group. The most commonly designated subraces of the Caucasoid stock are Nordic, the people of northern Europe; Alpine, the people of central Europe; Mediterranean, the people of southern Europe; and Armenoid, the people of the Near East. The subdivision of the inhabitants of an area such as Europe, within which there are no major barriers to migration or movement of genes, is an arbitrary division of a continuum, and there are no sharp boundaries between the different subdivisions.

Physical anthropologists agree that the diversity of modern man can be explained only as a result of the processes of evolution. As any two populations of animals that are separated from each other tend to diversify in physical characteristics as a result of adaptation to different environments, so mankind must have diversified because of natural selection and other evolutionary processes. The majority of physical characteristics that vary regionally in modern man are now thought to be characteristics that were related to adaptive advantages to specific environments in times past. Since, however, man relates to his environment through culture, traits that were advantageous in the past do not necessarily remain so in terms of today's culture. The revolution of food production, which changed man's entire relationship to nature, and the industrial revolution, which was related to the conquest of many environmental and health problems by means of technology, occurred too recently to have been reflected as yet in man's physical makeup. It is likely that natural selection still operates, but the manner in which it operates can change with the cultural situation. In the past, natural selection might have favored the individual with superior resistance to epidemic diseases or with the ability to survive on very little food; selection in modern America, on the other hand, may single out those with superior resistance to radiation or to psychological pressures. Men of ten thousand years in the future will probably be different in physical characteristics from the men of today, but it is impossible to predict in what features the differences will appear.

Diagrams 1 and 2 are intended to represent schematically the change of thinking about the physical diversity of man that has taken place in physical anthropology. Diagram 1 represents the older conception of races as separate entities that overlapped very little or not at all. Diagram 2 represents modern thinking, which emphasizes that man is a single species varying between extremes. Although an individual located near the edge of one of the lobes in Diagram 2 will look quite different from someone near the edge of a different lobe, there will exist a continuum of persons intermediate in characteristics between them.

Inherent in the old system of classification was the idea that in the past there were "pure" races, the members of which looked very much alike; therefore, the individual of today who does not correspond to one of the hypothetical pure types is considered to be the result of interbreeding. Connected with this idea was the belief that racial characteristics were nonadaptive and that races were stable and unaffected by evolution. Today, populations are considered to differ as a result of the processes of evolution acting upon physical characteristics that were adapted for particular environments. No ideal or pure types are postulated in modern racial theory, for the unit of operation is the population, and all populations are known to be variable. The old school of physical anthropology worked at attempting to trace people back to the earlier pure races. The result was usually the creation of additional ideal types in an effort to accommodate the many individuals who did not fit the established classifications. Modern physical anthropologists concentrate upon the objective comparison of populations and seek answers through a better understanding of the mechanisms of evolution.

One matter that must be discussed is the question of differences in ability, intelligence, or temperament between races. A great deal of ill will, prejudice, and persecution has been based upon the assumption that some groups of people are "naturally" inferior to other groups. The case that comes to mind most readily for modern readers is that of Negroid-Caucasoid relationships in the United States, but racial prejudice, although far from universal in human societies, has existed at many other times and places. Can physical anthropology make a definitive statement about inherent equality or inequality of men of different races?

A careful distinction must be made between the effects of heredity and environment in determining human capabilities. Differences in results on intelligence tests, in crime rates, or in average times in the 100-yard dash can exist between groups, whether the groups are those of different races, different religions, or different areas of the country. The important point in organizing societal action is whether the differences are genetic, and therefore almost unalterable, or whether they are the result of different backgrounds and opportunities. If, for example, slum-dwellers have inborn criminal tendencies, a social agency could not use the same program to alter crime rates that it would use if slum-dwellers were merely the victims of unwholesome surroundings.

DIAGRAM 1   DIAGRAM 2

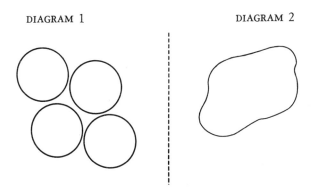

Since no test has ever been devised that can separate heredity from environmental factors, no final statement can be made about whether or not all racial groups are exactly alike in all respects. It is easy, however, to demonstrate that background plays a large role in social behavior and capability and that no clear case of hereditary racial differences in these areas has ever been demonstrated. An assumption to which almost all anthropologists would subscribe is that if any inherited differences exist between groups, they are minor compared to the effects of environmental differences.

Suggested Readings

Garn, Stanley M., *Readings on Race*. Springfield, Ill.: Charles C. Thomas, Publisher, 1959. A collection of articles emphasizing the processes of race formation.

McKern, Thomas W., *Readings in Physical Anthropology*. Englewood Cliffs, N.J.: Prentice-Hall, Inc., 1966. A selection of readings including many viewpoints from recent physical anthropologists.

UNESCO, *The Race Concept*. Paris: UNESCO, 1951, New York: Columbia University Press, 1952. A consideration by leading scientists of the problem of race and cultural capability.

5

THE NATURE OF CULTURE

The nature of culture has been explored in the beginning chapters by study of the biological base for human behavior and through the story of the prehistoric development of culture. The concept of culture has been introduced by a glimpse of what physical anthropology and archeology have contributed. In the ensuing chapters, culture is examined from the viewpoint of cultural anthropology. This approach derives its findings from the study and comparison of present-day cultures. Thorough description of other peoples' ways of life depends upon the development of objective field-work techniques. The comparison of these cultures follows scientific methodology with particular anthropological adaptations.

The method of cultural anthropology

Anthropologists in the nineteenth century depended largely on the reports of missionaries, explorers, and government officials. The bias of these reports soon made it obvious that anthropologists would have to gather their own data. At the turn of the century expeditions began, and it became traditional that a cultural anthropologist spent part of his training period in the field.

Gradually, techniques developed that made possible the collection of reliable data. Field work in another culture is carried out over a year or longer in order to study activities during the various seasons. Months must be spent in building rapport with a people to discover intimate activities and subtle beliefs. Rapport is built by learning the people's language, living much as they do, and helping in small ways such as giving first-aid or simply providing aspirin tablets. As much as possible, one participates in the culture under study while making all sorts of observations. Thus, the major technique of cultural anthropology is known as *participant observation*. On occasion, the anthropologist may have to limit his work to the administration of questionnaires or to the *survey method*. Ideally, the survey method is a supplement to participant observation.

The major advantage that the anthropological fieldworker has over the missionary or government worker is in his perspective. The anthropologist lives in another culture with a strong respect for *culture relativity*. He judges behavior and beliefs in terms of the culture in which they occur. He does not condemn infanticide or polygamy but seeks to discover how and why these practices developed. Secondly, he attempts to understand the culture he studies as a *whole*. Although field-work techniques provide guidelines, what an anthropologist collects depends in part on his personality and interests. Two anthropologists in the same culture do not "see" exactly the same things because of their different backgrounds. Thus, field work must be recognized as partly subjective. Data from other cultures are also organized partly in terms of a particular culture but also along the lines of interest of particular anthropologists.

Although it may be difficult to make comparisons between cultures, *cross-cultural comparison* has become the method of modern anthropology. "Experiments" can be performed that parallel the method of the chemist or physicist. In a scientific problem, one factor correlates with and is believed to cause something else. In the laboratory, different factors can be manipulated singly or in combinations to discover which ones are really causal. Can the same technique be applied to man's behavior?

Early in the century it was believed that much of juvenile delinquency and other teen-age problems were caused by the biological changes of adolescence. Social scientists began to challenge this notion but were unable to prove their contentions because in America biological change and adolescent turmoil occurred together. However, Margaret Mead made a study of Samoa and found that biological adolescence did not cause problems there. Children easily made the transition to adulthood, assuming an important place in society during their teens. In short, the biological change of adolescence did not cause social or behavioral adjustment problems. A comparison of cultures made it possible to control a behavioral factor and to show that the cause was not linked with biology.

This case is useful to show how the comparison of cultures or the cross-cultural approach parallels experimental techniques in the laboratory. Furthermore, it is an illustration of a trend in social science. Formerly, much of behavior was explained as instinct. Now emotions and even outlook on life are seen as the result of the ways in which culture determines relationship to environment, to other people, and to the supernatural. A "maternal instinct," a "drive for success," a "need for recognition" are no longer understood as being rooted in the psyche of man; rather, such behavior is interpreted in terms of cultural background.

Language and culture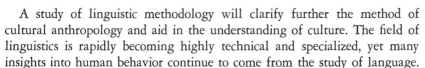

A study of linguistic methodology will clarify further the method of cultural anthropology and aid in the understanding of culture. The field of linguistics is rapidly becoming highly technical and specialized, yet many insights into human behavior continue to come from the study of language.

The first task of the linguist is to record, describe, and classify sounds. These steps are called *phonetics*. The task is not nearly as simple as it appears, because a person probably never makes any sound twice in exactly the same way; no two people make exactly the same sound. Of course, sounds are made so much alike that they are readily understood to be the same. For example, "democracy" consists of nine basic sounds with nine letters representing them. The many millions of English speakers familiar with the word vary slightly in their production and combination of sounds for this word; yet, despite variation, they always recognize what others mean.

Ideally, a linguist should be able to discriminate so finely in recording that he could describe the minute variation among all speakers. Such an ability seems impractical at present, but an example illustrates the importance of fine discrimination. Most people assume that the letter *p* in English stands for only one sound, and they will readily purse their lips to demonstrate the sound. However, if one holds his finger in front of his lips and says "pin" and then "spin," he will note that he breathes much harder on his finger when he explodes the *p* in "pin" than the *p* in "spin." In phonetics the two *p*'s must be assigned different symbols. In fact, there is a third phonetic symbol for *p* in English. If one says "lamp mat," he may observe a difference in the final *p* of lamp from the *p*'s in pin and spin.

A number of sounds vary in the same way, such as the *b* in "about" and "bound." However, linguists found that these sounds always vary in English according to certain rules. The degree to which a *p* is exploded depends upon the sounds immediately before and/or after it. These surrounding sounds are called the *environment*. The linguist can formulate rules that

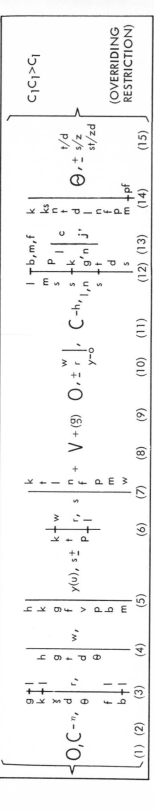

FIGURE 10. PHONEMES

The formula illustrates how phonemes can be combined in a monosyllabic word in English. By age five or six, English-speaking children have the formula completely ingrained.

specify in what types of environment each of the *p's* will occur. If a rule can be written for a variety of sounds, the different sounds are grouped into one unit called a *phoneme*. Phonemic analysis reduces the number of symbols yielded by phonetics.

All English speakers "learn" the phonemic rules of their language, and yet no one is ever "taught" them. Except for linguists, no one is aware of them. Neither parents nor teachers have ever explained to children that they must explode the *p* in "pin" more heavily than in "spin." Nonetheless, English-speaking children always learn to make such a discrimination in their speech.

The linguist has found similar rules, ones "learned but not taught," for the combination of phonemes into *morphemes* or words. (A morpheme is not exactly a word, but a precise definition is not needed here.) For instance, no English morpheme ever begins with the sound represented by *ng* as in "sing." This *ng* is a phoneme or single sound; it is not two sounds as it is spelled. Also, the sound represented by *s* in "measure" is never used initially in a morpheme.

The rules for combining phonemes within words become highly complex. (Figure 10) For example, the *l* phoneme never follows the *sh* phoneme in English. Thus, English speakers would recognize *schlafen*, the German verb meaning "to sleep," as a "foreign" word because it violates the rule. However, as the term "Schlitz beer" becomes more frequently used in English, speakers of the language may come to consider *shl* as native to their language.

Finally, the linguist is concerned about the combination or sequence of morphemes. The analysis of morpheme combinations is called *syntax*. Syntax is similar to grammar, but some of the rules of syntax discovered by linguists are not found in traditional grammar books. Possibly morphemes combine or pattern in ways much like phonemes; linguists have yet to analyze syntax as thoroughly as phonemes.

The study of language has had many important consequences. Linguists have shown that language is necessary for the learning and transmittal of culture. Children could not learn the culture of their parents without language. The essentials of democracy or Christianity, for example, could hardly be communicated without language. Other primates have been prevented from achieving cultural adaptations mainly because they lack speech. The utterances of a gorilla are standardized; sound always has the same meaning. Moreover, the number of meaningful sounds is limited, and they seem always to refer to a present emotional state. In human language one sound can have several meanings, and sounds can be combined to symbolize an infinite number of meanings. Human language can convey feelings about the past and future as well as the present; moreover, much more than an emotional state can be communicated. The symbols of man not only reveal present emotions but also can be used to evoke feelings in others. Man's complex social life seems possible only because he is able to create in someone else feelings analogous to his own. Communication of this sort allows common goals and values and thus a group life of a highly complex nature.

Further, the analysis of language also demonstrated how frequently learning was acquired in the same way English speakers learn that words never begin with the *ng* phoneme or that certain combinations of phonemes are impossible. Linguists focused attention on all sorts of behavior acquired in the same informal way that a child learns to explode a *p* in one context but not in another.

At first thought, an English speaker will claim there is no difference in the way he says: the Green house (in contrast to Mr. Brown's house), the green house (as opposed to the yellow one), or the greenhouse (where flowers are grown). However, one may experiment with a friend, using the three phrases as the subject of a sentence. One finds that the speaker does discriminate between the three by use of certain stresses and pauses. Moreover, his listener will be able to discriminate in the same way.

The importance of this phenomenon for the study of culture should be clear. If so much of language is transmitted unknowingly, then how much of culture is learned in the same way? Of how much of our behavior are we really aware? Until linguists achieved accuracy in their methods, no one fully understood many of the existing rules in language, even though grammarians had been studying the language for decades. Anthropologists wonder how many rules of behavior are still to be uncovered.

The second major contribution of linguistics has been continual emphasis upon the patterning of language. In the study of phonetics it soon became clear that all peoples have chosen for their languages only a few of the many possible sounds they could make. In constructing phonemes of these sounds, they followed consistent rules; that is, they patterned their language. In the study of morphemes and especially of syntax, patterning is even more apparent. English sentences, for example, are patterned in that they have an actor and act or a subject and verb; occasionally what is acted upon (the object of the verb) is included or implied. For instance, one "shrugs" his shoulders; one never shrugs his stomach. Any additions to the sentence simply elaborate upon the basic pattern.

Another important element in the pattern is that time of action is expressed. Verbs change according to the time when the action is taking place. Strangely, for all the concern with the future among most English speakers, the future tense requires an addition, such as "will" or "shall," and the past tense generally involves only an internal change in sound or the "ed" ending. In other languages the pattern may differ radically. For instance, in Navajo the verb changes, not to express time, but in accord with the object. If the object is soft and flat (like a blanket, for example) the verb will have one form; if the object is hard and round, the verb will have another form. In the Eskimo pattern, little distinction is made between actor and action. "I do not know" is translated as "not-knowing-am-I-it."

In summary, the important contributions of linguistics for cultural analysis are (1) the demonstration of how extensively behavior can be acquired informally or unknowingly and (2) the ways in which language is patterned. These two points will be discussed later but are most useful for introducing the study of culture.

Taxonomy of culture

In addition to the insights about culture provided by linguistic analysis, anthropologists clarified the concept by classifying culture in different ways. Several categories or divisions of culture have been devised. These categories have yielded various insights into the nature of culture; future classifications will doubtless add new insights.

One simple scheme is to divide culture into its *material* and *nonmaterial* aspects. Material culture includes such things as foods, tools, and house types; nonmaterial culture is composed, in part, of beliefs, values, and ideologies. The division poses such interesting problems as rate of change. Which changes more rapidly, material or nonmaterial culture? A theory stemming from this question postulates that innovations in material culture are inevitable. Once a particular level of technology is reached, certain inventions and discoveries must follow, and hundreds of simultaneous innovations have been recorded. However, there is no evidence that nonmaterial culture changes in the same way. Nonmaterial culture generally must change to adapt to innovations in material culture, but the nonmaterial change follows the material one. The difference in rate between the two is termed *culture lag.* The concept of culture lag is useful for understanding why Americans may drive next year's cars by yesterday's traffic laws. The cars are a part of material culture; legislation is part of nonmaterial culture.

Culture has also been divided into categories of *ideal* and *real.* Ideal culture is what people believe or would like culture to be; real culture is what actually exists. For instance, many critics of American life have pointed out the hypocritical standards of equality and the actual treatment of racial or ethnic groups. The difference between actual and ideal sex behavior has also been noted. Critics generally fail to understand that one frequently finds differences between what people say "should be" (or the *norms*) and what they do. Some discrepancies between norms and behavior occur in all cultures. In short, man everywhere finds it impossible to practice what he preaches.

An understanding of the difference between ideal and real culture led social scientists to more intensive observation. It is not possible just to ask people how or why they behave the way they do; such questions elicit only ideal culture. Anthropologists had to participate and closely observe behavior in other cultures before they could be confident of recording real culture as well as ideal culture. Moreover, the understanding that real culture frequently differs from the ideal opened new problems. What is the relationship between real and ideal culture? How does change in one affect the other? How wide a gap can there be between the two? In addition to provoking questions, the concept of real and ideal culture provided new insights. The relationship between norms and behavior has been clarified to a major degree. This contribution is of great importance, and much attention is now given to the influence of actual behavior upon the norms and of the norms upon real behavior.

A third useful breakdown of culture into simpler parts was developed by historical anthropologists. In their study, they often concentrated on a single, isolated unit called a cultural *trait*. For example, much time was spent in tracing the distribution of outrigger canoes in the South Pacific. Similarities in outrigger construction were used to demonstrate previous connections between people. The more similarities that could be found, the more of the past would be revealed; therefore, the historical anthropologists added units closely related to their original trait. Along with outrigging went such traits as shape of hulls and sails and techniques of building and navigation. It became obvious that sets of traits were closely related; these sets were called *trait complexes*.

The historical method led to the mistaken conception of culture as historical accident. However, trait complexes were eventually grouped in a larger unit termed a *pattern*. Anthropologists once postulated a universal culture pattern with components of speech, material traits, art, mythology, religion, family, property, government, and war. This list was much discussed and criticized for omissions. In the end it was found to be of little theoretical use, but the categories of trait, trait complex, and pattern proved especially valuable in the ordering of data. Museums arranged collections according to the scheme, and cultural anthropologists were provided a better means for organizing their descriptions.

Patterning of culture

The major contribution arising from trait complex and pattern analysis was the stimulus given to anthropologists who used the concept of pattern to provide insight into the nature of culture. The idea of a universal pattern suggests that culture is much more than the product of borrowing or diffusion of traits and independent invention. Anthropologists began to understand that man everywhere faces certain common problems if he is to live in groups, accumulate knowledge, and transmit what he has learned. Behavior must be organized to solve the problems of group life and cultural adaptation. Solutions to these problems resulted in a number of universal adaptations and gave rise to patterning.

A major adaptation of man has been the replacement of biological change with tools, fire, shelter, and other traits of material culture. For instance, the use of weapons meant that man no longer depended on his teeth for fighting or hunting; canines were reduced in size or never developed as they did in most primates. As pointed out previously, man everywhere has used material culture in adjusting to his environment. Culture has allowed him to exploit even poisonous food sources. Fire, clothing, and shelter have enabled him to move into all parts of the world. Food producing, a major cultural adaptation, provided for a population increase unimaginable by means of biological change. The cultural adaptations have been such that some generalizations can be made about ways in which man everywhere has reacted in making such adaptations. Notably, man everywhere has made similar adjustments to his physical environment, to group life, and to the supernatural.

Man has organized his food quest and other interrelations with physical environment in such a way that all cultures may be said to have *economic systems*. That is, the production, distribution, and consumption of goods have been organized or systematized everywhere. (Figure 11) These economic processes are never accomplished by individuals, in contrast with most species, but by specialized groups within the larger group. Furthermore, man has always elaborated upon the organization; the economic system does much more than simply meet the needs of hunger or protection. In all cultures food, clothing, and housing are used to indicate status, to symbolize religious beliefs, and to allow the expression of aesthetic feelings.

Other universal cultural adaptations may be seen in man's interaction with other men. Social life creates many problems. Man has devised an amazing variety of techniques to govern social relations, but everywhere some similar adjustments have been made. In all cultures, rules exist that divide work between the sexes and between generations, although each culture has a different view of which tasks are assigned to whom. There are many cultures in which things we consider "women's work" are done by men, and in other cultures women perform arduous and dangerous labor that we consider appropriate only for men. Nevertheless, it is striking that everywhere males are a separate social group from females.

Similarly, tasks, duties, and privileges are always divided between young and old. In part, such division springs from the fact that all societies must *enculturate* children (transmit culture to them). (Figures 12, 13) Rules must exist to define the relationship between adults and youth, although these rules vary greatly. The young may be considered to have greater power than the adults, or the aged may be considered most wise and the ultimate authority. However, the important point is that norms exist in all cultures

FIGURE 11. THE MARKET-PLACE

In Nigeria, a market place exchange system operates quite like that in the United States, but on a much smaller scale. Women are often the major vendors.

defining the relationship between generations. Thus, all societies demonstrate defined or structured social relations between the sexes and between generations.

In addition to environmental and social adaptations, all cultures have established some relationship with the supernatural. This relationship may pervade almost all of a culture, or it may be quite compartmentalized. It may be largely a matter of individual concern, or it may be a communal activity. Although the form it takes may vary widely between different cultures, all peoples have developed some kind of religion. It is probable

FIGURE 12. FAMILY GROUP

In all cultures, much of the enculturation takes place in the context of the family.

FIGURE 13. MOTHER AND CHILD

An African woman beginning the enculturation of her child. Attitudes and an outlook on life are conveyed by parents to a child from the time of birth.

that some individuals in all cultures question this relationship; certainly there is a range of intensity of belief in all cultures. What is striking is that all cultures have established relations with the supernatural. The adaptations of man to environment, to social life, and to the supernatural are patterned relationships. Ruth Benedict made a major contribution to the social sciences by demonstrating the pattern of culture in three particular cultures. Moreover, she provided insight into the ways patterning arises because of the relationship between personality and culture. For instance, if children are reared to control their emotions and to place group interests before their own, then cooperation, inoffensiveness, sobriety, and similar values will pattern behavior in adaptations to environment, to other people, and to the supernatural.

People, like the Pueblo Indians, who own land in common and exploit it communally are going to emphasize cooperation in their man-to-man relationships. Similarly, their gods are not likely to be seen as highly competitive figures; rather, the religion emphasizes the morality of working together. In short, most of the learned, shared behavior (culture) takes on a pattern of group harmony demanding subordination of individuality. The emphasis upon group life pervades economic, social, political, and religious behavior. (Figure 14)

The concept of culture patterning demonstrates how the various parts of culture parallel each other. Another important fact about culture is that the various parts are *integrated* with each other.

Form, meaning, and function

Ways in which culture is integrated may be illustrated by one of the methods for describing cultural traits. A Pueblo house, for instance, might be described as an architect would see it. Photographs, floor plans, and a description of building materials would illustrate one aspect of a pueblo. This aspect is called *form*. Knowing the forms of a trait helps in a study of diffusion. The remains available to an archeologist are generally described by form. However, the cultural anthropologist can also determine what a pueblo *means* to a Zuni or a Hopi Indian. It can be determined if the house is a place of both secular and sacred activities or if the house is closely associated with the idea of family life. The meaning of a trait is inferred in part by observation, but anthropologists determine meaning largely by asking people how they feel about a trait. Finally, the *functions* of a trait may be described. Some functions, called *manifest*, are obvious to the people using a trait. The Pueblo house, for instance, provides a place for storage of household items and protection against rain and cold. Any Pueblo Indian understands these functions. However, the Pueblo house also functions in promoting the values of group harmony and cooperation. The upkeep of one house influences many other houses; the proximity of houses demands that families remain on fairly close terms at all times. The functions of Pueblo housing in promoting and supporting prime cultural values are not apparent to the people. These functions are called *latent*; they are discovered by the analysis of social scientists.

Analysis by form, meaning, and function may be applied to nonmaterial culture as well. The form of the American family consists of the relations between spouses, between parents and children, and between brothers and sisters. The meaning of the family would be described in terms of what individuals think of family life. Sociologists have emphasized that for Americans the family means security and a source of emotional life. "Togetherness" is another aspect of meaning for the family.

Examples of manifest functions for the family are reproduction, rearing of children, and control of sexual behavior. A latent function of the family

FIGURE 14. INDIAN DANCERS

The Eagle dancers of New Mexico's Laguna Indian Pueblo. This ceremony shows at a glance an emphasis upon cooperation and harmony, values explicit in all Pueblo relationships, including the supernatural.

is social control. The single person can question or break the rules of society more easily than married persons because he is the only one to be punished. However, a husband must fear punishment not only for himself but also for his family. Of course, Americans are aware that their families may suffer from their acts, but they do not ordinarily think of family life as one means of enforcing the norms of society.

The form of the American family can also be built through description of traits and trait complexes. However, a description of the form of the family as consisting of parents and children reveals only ideal culture. Although most families are of such form, some include other relatives or exclude one of the parents. Thus, real culture is somewhat different from ideal culture; the differences between ideal and real culture are of particular importance for a discussion of the meaning of family life.

Functional theory

As theory developed, "function" acquired two meanings. As this term was defined above, it meant the way in which material or nonmaterial culture fulfilled certain needs. One asks how a trait or trait complex functions to satisfy biological, psychological, or social needs. However, another meaning of function has to do with the integration of cultural parts. For instance, a complete analysis of American family function would include a description of how the independence of newly married couples makes possible a mobile population and how this mobility provides the labor force for modern industrial and urban life. It is not possible to discuss the American family fully without also analyzing the American economic system. Similarly, American religion, politics, and education are also tied to the family. What develops from such functional analysis is an emphasis upon the integration of many parts of culture. Parts can only be explained in terms of the whole culture.

An English anthropologist, A. R. Radcliffe-Brown, was largely responsible for emphasizing the meaning of integration in functional thought. To paraphrase him, function is the contribution of one activity to all activity. The function of a particular trait is the part it plays in the total social system. A social system has a unity that may be spoken of as "functional unity."

The double connotation involved in functional theory presents difficulties, but the two meanings of functionalism are mutually dependent. Some understanding would be lost if the definition was sharply limited simply for precision. The interdependence of the two meanings may be understood through an analogy with biology. Life consists of many cells in a particular arrangement known as a structure. For life to persist, a continuity of the structure must be maintained while each part performs certain functions. One part assimilates oxygen, another absorbs food, and so on. Each part is interdependent on all the others; if one were to cease functioning, all the others would be endangered. In short, the function of one part is to meet a particular need; at the same time, the part is functionally dependent on the other systems. For example, the circulatory system carries food and oxygen provided by the digestive and respiratory systems.

Functional theory emphasizes the integrated complexity of biological life. Functional theory in anthropology emphasizes how various aspects of culture fulfill various needs for society and its members and how at the same time the parts are linked so that they cannot be changed without affecting the rest of culture.

Culture change

Functional theory has had an important influence upon the study of culture change, but to understand the theory's effect, the field of culture change as a whole should be reviewed. Anthropologists long recognized that analysis of culture change revealed how different parts of a culture worked and how parts fitted together. Moreover, a comparison of the same culture at two different points in time made available a more refined control of factors. The effects of industry on society may be examined by comparing some tribal groups with English or French culture, the usual cross-cultural approach. Another method is to compare pre-Industrial England with current England. In the latter case, the comparative method is being practiced, but only one culture is examined.

The first system for understanding culture change was developed by the earliest anthropologists, the social evolutionists. They postulated long-term changes in culture based largely on speculation. Various schemes were devised to explain the evolution of the family, religion, politics, law, and other areas of human development. One grand scheme saw the evolution of man through stages of savagery (hunting) to barbarism (simple agriculture) to civilization. The social evolutionists tried too many broad generalizations with far too little data, but they focused attention on the subject of culture change.

The next theorists concerned themselves with empirical studies of change over short periods. Analysis focused primarily on traits and how they spread or *diffused*. In fact, some cultures were largely explained as the result of diffusion; cultures were described by examination of the many borrowings that had built them. Of course, the origin of traits had to be explained, and anthropologists concerned themselves with the phenomenon of invention. Much controversy centered on whether man was fairly inventive and through independent invention had developed similar traits or whether he depended largely on a few geniuses whose inventions were widely spread. For instance, both the Maya and the Egyptians built pyramids. Those who held the view that man was largely uninventive argued that the idea of pyramid building must have diffused from the Old World to the New World because the Maya pyramids are much later in time. As illustration of how form, meaning, and function analysis proved useful, it might be pointed out that the Maya pyramids must have been independently invented because only the forms are similar. The meaning and function of the Maya and Egyptian pyramids are completely different. (Figure 15)

The debate over the merits of diffusion versus independent invention kept interest in culture change alive. Anthropology documented the spread of numerous traits and recorded much of the history of contacts of little known peoples. However, the interest narrowed anthropological perspective. During this period little attention was paid to the effects of Western and Oriental cultures on the other peoples of the world. Anthropologists wrote reports of their field work in other cultures as if the cultures existed before contact with the modern world. In short, anthropologists were ignoring the culture change that was occurring right before their eyes.

However, the oversight was soon corrected. A major emphasis in the 1930's was placed on the recording of the effects of the modern world on other people. Whereas former anthropologists had studied the exchange of

FIGURE 15. PYRAMIDS

The Egyptian and Mayan pyramids are alike in form, but the meaning and function differ. The Maya form is no longer considered to have diffused from Egypt.

traits on a small scale (diffusion), anthropologists now turned their attention to the major changes wrought by intensive contact and large-scale exchange. This process was called *acculturation*. Acculturation was defined as what occurs when groups having different cultures come into prolonged contact, thereby changing the culture patterns of one or both groups. The process always affects all groups involved but generally affects some more than others. Anglo-American contact with American Indians brought many changes to the latter. Indian influence on Anglo culture was less noticeable although much more significant than most Americans realize.

The study of culture change has become a subfield within anthropology. Space is not available here to introduce the field systematically or to develop the technical vocabulary. Examination of a few of the problems in this field should give some insight into the nature of culture, however.

The study of acculturation reveals that the form of a trait complex is generally exchanged much more readily than are its meaning and function. People coming into extensive contact with the Western world have often had to exchange their former livelihoods for wage labor. (Figures 16, 17, 18) Acculturation so affected American Indians and is now important in Africa. Indians and Africans quickly adapted to the practice of exchanging labor for money, something alien to their former way of life. The meaning of wage labor is quite complex; Western man values work in itself, and to be self-respecting he must continually work for a living. This meaning of work is well expressed in parts of the Bible and in many of our proverbs. However, the value of work for its own sake has never passed easily to other cultures. As a result, the Indian or African has often worked for wages just long enough to acquire from the other group the few material items he deems valuable. The meaning of work is fundamentally different, so obviously the function of work must be different.

Another problem in culture change was to determine what areas of behavior were most and least likely to change. Early studies of culture change indicated that in acculturation a society's economy was likely to change rapidly while religion persisted. Attempts were made to outline these areas and their order of change. In general, change occurs first in economy, then in social relations such as the family and politics. Forms of religion, basic values, and personality resist change longest. However, a number of exceptions to this sequence were soon discovered. In some cultures religion is quickly discarded and economy remains. Study of the exceptional cases indicated that religion in these cultures was not rigorously taught to young children; major religious instruction occurred in adolescence or early youth. Further analysis led to the conclusion that those areas of behavior learned early in life are most persistent in acculturation. This statement helps to explain why some parts of culture are more likely to be taken for granted or to be less susceptible to question.

FIGURE 16. SURVEYING

Cultural diffusion from industrial to less developed nations is a commonplace in the world of today. Here, American engineers instruct Arab trainees in surveying.

FIGURE 17. MACHINIST IN SUMATRA

Western technology and the demand for industrial jobs have diffused around the world. Although people in other cultures quickly learn the skills, they may fail to accept work habits, money values, and other features of Western ideology.

Acculturation studies soon made it apparent that anthropology might alleviate many of the human problems that develop when cultures come in contact. During World War II, many peoples suddenly found themselves involved with Western culture. In the Pacific, for instance, many island peoples were thrown in close contact with Japanese, Australians, and Americans. After the war these people, as well as many in Africa and Southeast Asia, found they were now part of the modern world and could not revert to their former ways of life. New technologies, health practices, political and religious ideologies seriously disrupted hundreds of cultures. Anthropologists were asked how such innovations could spread with a minimum of disruption. The answers provided by anthropology and other social sciences are still not complete, but the study of culture change has con-

FIGURE 18. RAILROAD BUILDING IN NIGERIA

Another example of the spread of Western technology is pictured here. Workers are relaying a section of track under the railway development program in Nigeria.

tributed much to easing the human problems involved in acculturation. The application of culture-change theory led to the development of a new field called *applied anthropology*.

With the development of applied anthropology, the study of culture change over short periods has become more precise and has led to applications and testing of theory, but the analysis of long-term change has been relatively neglected. Recently, however, emphasis upon long-term change has revived, and the early works of social evolutionists are being re-evaluated. Although many faults of these initial ideas in anthropology are obvious, it seems likely that some of the evolutionist's basic suppositions were correct. Regularities in culture growth have been noted as man changed from food gatherer to food producer, and comparative studies of the beginning of civilization in the New and Old Worlds reveal some striking uniformities. Unlike the older social evolutionists who insisted on one precise path of advance, the "neo-evolutionists" speak of *multilinear* cultural growth. That is, mankind has followed several different paths in social evolution, but there are similarities among these paths. One fruitful approach in analysis of the similarities is a concentration upon the ways in which man has increased the efficiency of using energy or of discovering new energy sources. Another approach has been the comparative evolution of the complexity of social life.

In summary, it must be emphasized that a functional description generally implies a static culture. As the pattern of a culture is laid out by an ethnographer or as a social anthropologist integrates the many different parts of a culture, little room is left for the possibility of change. Yet cultures are always changing and have always done so. The study of culture change has not negated the idea of patterning nor destroyed the concept of functionalism. It has demanded that culture be seen as dynamic. Ethnographic accounts have improved as they concentrate on how parts of a culture change together rather than simply on how they fit together. The emphasis upon process rather than upon static description adds much to an understanding of the nature of culture.

Suggested Readings

Beattie, John, *Bunyoro: An African Kingdom* (Case Studies in Anthropology). New York: Holt, Rinehart & Winston, Inc., 1965. Beattie describes the techniques of his field work among the Bunyoro. He details the everyday life of an anthropologist in the field from housekeeping and learning a language to the procedures of collecting, analyzing, and presenting ethnographic data.

portant in anthropology. Although only basic elements of kinship are introduced, they illustrate how a science of man is developing.

DIAGRAM N. OMAHA TERMINOLOGY

Large kin groupings

Despite the large numbers of persons incorporated in a unilineal system
with sibs, some societies organize groups above the sib level. Sibs may be
linked together to form *phratries*. Generally, the bond between sibs is
rationalized in mythology. The myth does not postulate a common ancestor,
like the sib, but instead simply gives reasons why sibs are specially linked.
The link may mean particular cooperation of sibs on ceremonial occasions,
or it may go so far as to establish exogamous or endogamous rules for the
phratry. The functions of the phratry are not clearly understood, except
for its expansion of relationships beyond the sib level.

A grouping of sibs or phratries that results in a *dual organization* of
society is termed a *moiety*. Moiety organization divides society into two
parts. The population need not be equally divided, but the moieties are
given balanced powers. The results of moiety organizations are so distinctive
that when sibs are organized into only two groups, they are not called
phratries but rather moieties. Some features of moiety organizations are an
opposition in games and similar activities and relationships of boasting,
ridicule, and rivalry.

Although these features are well recognized by anthropologists and provide a further instance of regular, recurrent behavior, scientific analysis of moiety organization is far from complete. The causal factors of such behavior are largely unexplained, and the functions of moieties have been explored only to a limited extent. Moieties may serve a psychological purpose in reducing frustration by directing and controlling aggression, but this hypothesis has not been verified. A full understanding of moiety organization must await future work by anthropologists.

Voluntary groupings

Membership in a phratry or moiety is usually determined by kinship; one belongs to father's or mother's grouping. In some rare instances, order of birth may determine membership. The first-born is assigned membership in one moiety, the second-born in the other. Whatever the method, the individual does not make a choice, just as one does not choose his age, sex, or most of his kin. Such assigned places within society are termed *ascribed statuses*.

FIGURE 24. HOPI INDIAN CEREMONY

Among the Hopi Indians of Arizona, a series of men's associations are responsible for the ceremonial life of the village.

Every society has ascribed statuses; most also have *achieved statuses*. An individual either requests or earns these positions. The groups one chooses to join are *associations*. In Hopi culture the Kachinas are an association. (Figure 24) Examples of American associations are fraternities, a street corner gang, the Elks, the American Anthropological Association, or a political group such as that shown in Figure 25. Associations have tests of membership and may use age and sex criteria, but individuals are not born into them. Associations do not exhibit the regularity observed in kinship behavior, although they have such universal characteristics as limiting their membership and developing an *esprit de corps* or other feelings for binding members together. Interestingly, one of the most frequently used bonds is artificial kinship. Even in modern America, members of a fraternity are "brothers" and labor unions become "brotherhoods."

Stratification

In all societies some statuses are deemed more worth while than others. In some places it is better to be male than female or young than old. Achieved statuses almost always carry *prestige*, which is one important reason that

FIGURE 25. ASSOCIATION MEETING

In America, many men's associations are manifestly social and charitable, but associations are also important in most institutions, such as economic and political ones.

people seek them. Why statuses become ranked in certain ways is a subject for advanced work in social science. The answer depends upon much more than the importance of a status for society. In America, for instance, garbage collectors are probably as vital to the health of a community as are doctors; yet one status carries much prestige, the other little. (Figures 26, 27) An even better instance of the complexity of prestige assignment is the case of iron workers in Africa and Malaysia. In both places workers smelt iron ore and cast hoes, knives, and spearheads. Their contributions are almost identical. However, in Africa iron workers are looked on with contempt and usually must live outside the villages; in Malaysia they are highly valued and respected.

Whatever the reasons for ranking statuses, the process produces a sig-

FIGURE 26. CASTES IN INDIA

In India, social stratification is extremely rigid, resulting in castes. Castes are endogamous strata. Here, a caste mark is being placed on an upper caste member.

FIGURE 27. STRATIFICATION IN AMERICA

In America, occupation is an important part of stratification. What work a man does determines where he will live and what type of housing he will have. Few Americans would fail to link the businessmen with the top house.

nificant organization of people. Certain statuses are given about equal prestige. These categories of statuses make up groups defined as *social classes*. Social classes become an important feature of society as entire families are assigned class status dependent upon one of the members of the family, usually the husband-father. Thus, social class standing is an ascribed status for a child, but the individual may have to achieve his class status as an adult. The features of class organization have received close attention from sociology; anthropologists only recently have entered the field to any large degree.

Political organization

In their relationships, all peoples have developed customs that may be called political. The essence of political organization is the sharing of rights to a territory and the arranging of mutual services such as protection. From this activity stem recognition of common membership in a group, *esprit de corps*, and shared symbols. Further organization of the society as a whole, or by groups, results in *governing* bodies whose functions are *internal* (social control and welfare) and *external* (relations with other societies).

Anthropologists recognize political organization in all cultures, though such items as law codes, flags, or capitols may be lacking. The important aspect of politics is the occupation of a defined territory; the idea of sovereign area is common to all cultures. The tie to a territory is in large part ecological, as in other species, but for man this tie is supplemented by sentiment, myth, and religion as well. Not only is the territorial link well defined, but the relation to neighboring units is also clearcut. Even hunters and herders, who move frequently and over long distances, hold to well-known territorial rights.

In small groups or even in some large groups, political behavior acts generally along kinship lines. That is, political authority is vested in those persons who can claim authority because of their standing in a kin group. Kinship, as a means of organizing political behavior, can work well even in large societies. In some West African kingdoms of a million or more, political groups coincided closely with kin groups. Kinship principles were important in prewar Japan.

However, as societies grow in size and complexity, political groupings generally develop around factors such as military or administrative ability, wealth, religion, or a complex of factors. (Figures 28, 29) With growth, there also develops a separation of legislative, executive, and judicial functions. In simple forms of organization these functions are combined in one person or status.

What is striking about man's political organization is the remarkable similarity that exists in all cultures. The differences between an Eskimo band, an Indian tribe, and a European state are primarily quantitative. Ways of doing things differ considerably, but the things done are quite alike.

Summary

In studying the relationship of man to man, anthropolgy has concentrated upon the age and sex structure of society and given particular attention to the relations based upon kinship. The universality of a limited number of kinship systems focused a search for generalizations about kin behavior. This search has demonstrated the potential and limits of scientific investigation of human behavior. The closely related organizations of phratry and moiety have likewise received considerable study. The voluntary group or association is being examined.

In analysis of this behavior, the anthropologist finds himself working in conjunction with the sociologist. Also, the anthropologist is beginning to

FIGURE 28. NAVAJO INDIAN MEETING

The form of Western political systems has diffused to to many peoples who use them with different meaning and function. Here a group of Navajo Indians meet in New Mexico to arrange the use of tribal funds.

concentrate on the effects of stratification, a field sociologists had nearly monopolized previously. Finally, anthropologists are joining political scientists as both attempt to understand political organization through cross-cultural comparisons. The study of human grouping ties anthropology with a number of other disciplines.

FIGURE 29. FRANCOIS TOMBALBAYE

Political change is sometimes as rapid as material change. Francois Tombalbaye, first President and Prime Minister of The Republic of Chad, was reared in a tribal political system; now he heads a nation.

Suggested Readings

Lowie, Robert, *Social Organization*. New York: Holt, Rinehart & Winston, Inc., 1948. Most of the concepts and principles of social organization are defined in this work; moreover, the concepts are well illustrated by ethnographic example. The book is highly useful as a reference.

Murdock, George P., *Social Structure*. New York: The Macmillan Company, 1949. This work is also an excellent reference; it is the source for most definitions of different social groups. The book not only explains various types of organization but also indicates the kinds of correlations existing between institutions, such as marriage and residence rules, and different types of organizations such as lineages and moieties.

Schusky, Ernest, *Manual for the Analysis of Kinship*. New York: Holt, Rinehart & Winston, Inc., 1965. This workbook allows students to understand the different types of kinship systems with minimal guidance from an instructor. It consists of a series of exercises for students to complete in order to master the details of classification of kinship systems. Behavior and organizations closely linked with kinship are also explained.

8

MAN AND THE SUPERNATURAL

Magic and religion

A discussion of the supernatural requires introduction to some definitions and concepts. The initial definitions are of limited value, but an appreciation of meanings will develop with presentation of case materials. Different views of religion and magic preclude any precise definitions of even these two basic terms.

In general, magic has been regarded as man's attempt to control the universe by a set of acts. In this sense, magic parallels science; the world is a *natural* one of cause-and-effect relationships. The magician, like the scientist, seeks mastery of the causes in order to produce desired effects. Religion, on the other hand, involves a state of feeling, special experience, or belief. Religion is the establishment of a relationship with the supernatural forces.

In analysis of actual practices, however, it is often difficult to distinguish behavior as specifically religious or magical. Is the magician who sticks pins in a doll to bring death any more of a controlling agent than a Christian group that prays long hours to bring health to a fellow member? Certainly, in many Christian denominations prayers seem to compel the supernatural to act. Anthropologists have concluded that magic cannot be clearly separated from religion. Instead, they conceive a continuum from a pole of compulsion to one of rapport. Much of man's behavior toward the supernatural lies somewhere between the poles; it is a combination of magical and religious behavior.

Man's attempts to establish a relation with the supernatural may be understood more fully by examination of the ingredients of magic and religion. The magician generally employs *imitative* (or homoeopathic) and *contagious* magic. The reasoning in imitative magic is that like produces like. A doll resembling the victim is afflicted in the belief that similar harm can be wrought upon the individual. A hunter draws a picture of an animal in order to produce game; cave art in Paleolithic times is almost certainly imitative magic. In contagious magic a belonging of the afflicted person is sought and rites performed over it. Hair, fingernail clippings, clothing, even feces and urine are favorite personal items for a magician to work upon.

The use of cause-and-effect reasoning in magical behavior means that the magician must demonstrate his special powers. His proof may be physiological. He may tremble or have spasms, go into a trance, or handle fire. The abilities are probably linked with self-hypnosis or personality abnormalities. Frequently, a magician is "seized" by a power that speaks through him in an unknown tongue; upon recovery, he interprets what the power has said. Or the magician may simply resort to trickery. For instance, curing is frequently performed by sucking out of the body a feather, worm, stick, or other cause of infection.

When a magician does "fail," his failures may be rationalized, by believers, into successes. In a present day Sioux community, a magician had been paid to solve a murder. The murderer had not been identified; however, few community members felt that the magician had been unable to discover his identity. They believed instead that the knowledge had been kept secret because the magician had discovered that the murderer was a close relative of the man who paid to have the murder solved. Others believed that the magician feared to reveal his discovery for reasons known only to him. One person rationalized the case ingeniously by saying, "What's the use of his telling? The courts would never accept his evidence anyway." Thus, regardless of the truth, the magician was assumed by most to have been successful.

In addition to such rationalization there is always an element of logic in mystical belief. One anthropologist reports an incident in which a man sitting under a house built on poles was killed when the structure collapsed. Informants assured the anthropologist that this death was a case of witchcraft. The anthropologist pointed out that the wooden poles were termite-infested and weatherworn. He was met with the quite logical response, "But why should the house collapse at the particular moment when the man stopped to rest under it?"

Even more rational thought is found in religious behavior. All peoples divide culture into the *sacred* and *secular*. Such division is found everywhere, but a clearcut line between secular and sacred is sometimes hard to draw. A Mayan Indian may offer a prayer (sacred) while at the same time hoeing his corn (ordinarily a secular event). A witness in court (explicitly secular in American culture) must swear an oath on a Bible (obviously sacred) before giving testimony (usually about quite secular matters).

Sacred and secular

However, men everywhere do recognize a sacred-secular dichotomy. What marks the sacred? Case studies of many different cultures reveal that the sacred is charged with some kind of supernatural force. Among American Indians this force was termed *manitoo* by Algonkin speakers and *wakan* by those speaking Sioux. Among others the force may go unnamed. In some Christian sects the Holy Ghost has been conceived as this force, but most Christians recognize it only implicitly.

The force has been given explicit treatment by Oceanic peoples who call it *mana*, a word which anthropologists have adopted as their technical term. That is, the sacred in any culture is characterized by its possession of mana. Mana is a power, force, or influence, not a god or deity. The power may be invested permanently or temporarily in men, animals, even winds or rivers. The force is impersonal and can produce good as well as evil. It has been compared with electricity in its danger and use.

Mana and taboo

Because of mana's inherent danger, those unprepared for its handling must be warned. The "charged" object may be *tabooed* (another word from Oceania); restrictions or prohibitions are laid down to give warning of mana. In some Oceanic islands, chiefs were so charged with mana that common people could not touch them or even approach them. Frequently, mana was so great that certain footpaths were reserved for chiefs—that is, tabooed to commoners.

Another safety check involved the hiding of sacred items. Australian aborigines have painted stones, known as *churingas*, which are powerfully charged with supernatural power. (Figure 30) Only fully initiated adult men can even gaze on the churinga; just a few men dare handle the stones. For a woman or child to see the churinga would mean instant death. Among Plains Indians a sacred medicine bundle was owned by most tribes.

FIGURE 30. CHURINGA

*An example of Churingas, the sacred stones of some
Australian tribes that are so charged with mana that only
a few shamans can handle them.*

TOTEM STONE or CHURINGA.
Jella or Yelka (bulb) Totem (Bulb of *Cyperus rotundus*,
Linn.).
ARUNTA TRIBE, CHARLOTTE WATERS, CENT. AUSTRALIA.

FIGURE 31. MEDICINE PIPE

A medicine pipe decorated with sacred symbols was considered by the Plains Indians to have great supernatural power. In this picture the form persists with a more modern meaning and function.

(Figure 31) This bundle was opened on special occasions, but most of the year it was carefully hidden away. Each village of the Papago, a Southwest Indian tribe, usually had its sacred bundle stored in the desert some miles from the village. Again only a few qualified persons could approach the sacred item.

Finally, objects possessing mana may be given special markings to serve as a warning. The symbol calls for certain responses rather than for a general prohibition as in taboo. Thus, in the presence of a Cross or Star of David many people are circumspect in their behavior.

Shamans and priests

The handling of mana always calls for special qualification, such as being initiated or being male. Generally, requirements are even more stringent. These requirements can be met in one of two ways. An individual may experience divine revelation of his qualifications. He may dream, fall into a trance, speak in unknown tongues, or discover a curiously marked rock. In some way or other he suddenly finds himself capable of handling mana. Such an individual is called a *shaman*. (Figure 32) The word is derived from Siberia, where sacred leaders are suddenly seized with power to control mana. Peoples whose religion is carried on largely by a shaman are generally hunters and gatherers. Shamans are often referred to as magicians, but anthropologists now use the former term.

Among agricultural people, who can afford specialization, sacred matters are more often in the hands of *priests*. (Figures 33, 34) Unlike the shaman, a priest receives a long period of training and indoctrination. The priests' knowledge of the supernatural may center around astronomical, agricultural, or other phenomena. Whatever is central in their training, a complex system of knowledge and an organized priesthood for transmittal of the knowledge are involved. The anthropologist would say that most Christian denominations are headed by priests, but a few depend primarily upon shamans who receive a "call" from God.

Social evolutionary theories of religion

Early anthropological inquiry into religion began with the social evolutionists of the late nineteenth century. One of their prime objectives was to determine the origin of religion. Edward Tylor, known as the father of anthropology, developed one of the most comprehensive theories of religious evolution. His basic assumption was that early man sought explanations for the dual nature of existence. At death, phenomena such as breathing and movement cease. This change suggests that "life" or "soul" has left the body. In addition, dreams, visions, swoons, and comas suggest a phantom of the self, capable of existence outside the body. Tylor felt that primitive man was led to deduce the presence of a phantom soul to account for these phenomena. A further development of religion extended this idea to animals and then to nonliving objects.

Tylor's theory is known as *animism*. It assumes a rational or intellectual approach by man to the creation of religion, which is highly unlikely, but it accounts for the religious practices of most people of the world. Ghosts,

FIGURE 32. SHAMANS

Among many Southwestern Indian tribes, shamans per-
form curing ceremonies to rid patients of physical or
supernatural ills.

FIGURE 33. ROMAN CATHOLIC ORDINATION

Most American Christian denominations are served by priests. The illustration shows the formal ceremony which marks the end of the long period of training necessary to become a Roman Catholic priest.

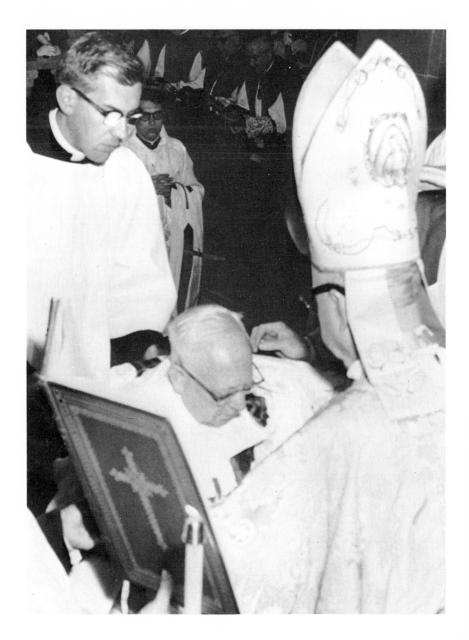

the transmigration of soul, and heavenly residences all follow from animistic theory.

Animism and theories growing out of animism can be given only brief treatment here. The simplification is unfair to the theorists; actually the various ideas are backed by considerable argument. Some of Tylor's and the early theorists' insights are remarkable, considering the scanty ethnographic materials then available.

Another evolutionist, Herbert Spencer, attempted to determine the origin of religion by looking at tribes considered the most primitive. The Australian aborigines were a favorite. Spencer believed that heroic ancestors were remembered by their descendants and gradually assumed godlike powers. Long-dead ancestors moved into the realm of the sacred. Much of the data from Australia supported this thesis. Spencer expresses the transition, saying the names of forebears became "capitalized" in the language. As the an-

FIGURE 34. BUDDHIST MONKS

In many non-Western religions, formal training is required for priests. Pictured here are Buddhist monks in Laos, participating in the opening ceremonies of the Buddhist Lent. Premier Souvanna Phouma (second from left) and Vice-Premier Prouni Nosavan (center) are giving offerings of food and flowers.

cestors form a community of souls, they became more and more identified as causal agents. Spirits are said to govern the weather, fortune, and even life itself. Such a view, called *manism*, sees man creating religion in part intellectually, in part emotionally. Spencer joins his theory of religion with his broader theory of society by pointing out that although fear of the living is basic in political control, fear of the dead is the foundation of religious control.

Another interesting explanation of religious origins was offered by Sir James Frazer. He argued, in the spirit of social evolution, that magic was older than religion because it is psychologically simpler. He claimed that magic, like science, assumed certain laws; the magician could control future events through knowledge of the laws. Unlike science, however, magic was invalid and often failed. After the repeated failure of magic, man finally bcame aware of his impotence and recognized a powerful force over which he had no control. When he prostrated himself before an all-powerful divine will, man had reached the stage of religion. Frazer postulated a final stage of science superseding religion, but he concentrated on the early developments in magic and religion. Most of his work is a study of world mythology published in a series of volumes called *The Golden Bough*. It has become one of the best known early anthropological works, although Frazer's theory was less influential than Tylor's.

The social evolutionists have been criticized extensively; social scientists today do not accept their theories. However, modern theorists have not solved the problem of origins; they have instead asked other questions. Interest now centers upon what religion does or how it works rather than on how it originated. The answers to these questions are based in part on ideas and concepts suggested by the social evolutionists. Evolutionary thought stimulated so much of current theory that this contribution alone makes the work of the social evolutionists valuable.

Historical theories of religion

As flaws appeared in the various theories of the social evolutionists, anthropology turned to the historical method. In the early twentieth century serious proposals were made that anthropology should be simply the historical study of people without written language. This trend meant an emphasis upon methods of reconstructing history where written records were absent. In large part, the field became a study of diffusion. One culture was linked to another by comparison of lists of traits; with much labor, paths of early trade and migration were traced. One grand scheme, however, developed from the work. Out of it new ideas on the nature of religion were to appear.

Father Wilhelm Schmidt, who trained many Catholic missionaries, believed that primeval man lived in small groups, possibly in Asia. As culture developed, migrations pushed out from the center. The earliest migrants would have been the most primitive, reaching remote areas of the world. Other bands would follow, eventually forming a pattern of cultural circles, *Kulturkreise*. Thorough study of trait complexes could reveal which cultures belong to which circles. For example, the Tasmanians and Pygmies are supposed to be related because of certain similarities. Schmidt, using the "earliest" circle, then reconstructed what must have been the earliest religion of man. He concluded that monotheism was first practiced, but later it was corrupted by animism. Thus, his view of religious origin is opposed to Tylor's. Although Schmidt's arguments are often weak and the *Kulturkreise* theory is no longer tenable, animism as an explanation of religion was no longer satisfactory. New hypotheses were sought in an attempt to account for religious behavior.

Psychological theories of religion

Some early psychologists explained religion quite easily by claiming it was instinctive. The basis of religion was attributed to a biological "primordial dread and anxiety" or to "self-preservation" or to "mystic experience." Little has been found to support any view that religion is based on instincts, but Freud and later psychologists have given much more sophisticated "psychological" reasons for religion.

In a search for origins, Sigmund Freud concluded that basic elements of religion stem from an act of patricide (killing a father). The primitive family was composed of mothers, father, and children much like a gorilla horde. In one of these groups the sons conspired to kill the father because of sexual jealousy over the mothers and sisters. After killing the father, they realized the horror of what they had done. They created incest taboos to prevent any recurrence of such an act and established totems to identify clearly all members of an exogamous group.

Freud's theory has been severely criticized by anthropologists and lacks any substantive evidence. However, Freud contributed much to the theory of religion in pointing out relationships between obsessive acts and religious practices. A good argument can be made that ritual in some societies probably stemmed from obsessional "rituals" developed in the lives of particular individuals. Just as a personal obsession relieves hidden anxiety for the individual, so certain ritual relieves stresses and anxieties felt by members of a society.

In focusing on a problem such as ritual behavior, Freud shifted interest from origins to the function of religion. Therefore, his work should be considered as part of the trend in the science of religion to examine the function rather than the origin of religion.

Functional anthropological theories of religion

The first functional analysis of religion is generally attributed to Emile Durkheim, whose views were published in *Elementary Forms of Religious Life* in 1912. Although Durkheim was concerned with religious origins, emphasis upon its function dominated his work.

In brief, Durkheim equated society with God. He pictured religion as a system of symbols justifying the values of society, thus making social life possible. To clarify the relation between society and religion, Durkheim analyzed the religious life of Australian aborigines. He believed the aborigines had an approximation of early religion; therefore, they would illuminate religious origins. The simpler system would be easier for analysis.

The argument, oversimplified, is that the sacred aspect of Australian religion centers on the totem, symbols of the sib. The totem's sacredness arises from the fact that it symbolizes the sib. Individuals unconsciously recognize that they cannot survive except as members of society. Unconsciously then, man recognizes that society is omnipotent, but in his expression of awe he creates a symbolic system that becomes religion. Totemism, for instance, is a religion according to Durkheim; the totem is nothing more than an unconscious symbol of the group known as a sib.

In gross simplification, Durkheim is saying that society deifies itself. This explanation of origin is intriguing but undemonstrated. Durkheim's major contribution lay in the elaboration of his theory. He noted that a group must maintain its solidarity by continuous moral support and reaffirmation. Religion, therefore, functioned to perpetuate society because it restricted individual whims on the one hand while providing common values, beliefs, and activities on the other.

Durkheim's theory directed the search for a hypothesis that would explain what types of social and psychological problems religion solves. Answers depended upon the cross-cultural examination of religion. What similarities are there in all religions, and what do these similarities do for the individual and for society? Two English anthropologists attacked these questions, and their answers remain the basis for much of current theory on religion.

Bronislaw Malinowski, in an intensive study of the Trobriand Islands, emphasizes what religion does for the individual. He maintains that all peoples have some empirical knowledge that might be called science. However, this knowledge is not powerful enough to insure all man's needs. The correct crops, soils, and tilling practices may be known and ordinarily provide sufficient food. But in some years, drought or storm prove more powerful than man. In such periods of stress, man turns to the supernatural. Malinowski's classic example centers on fishing practices. While fishing in calm lagoon waters, islanders can use an easy and reliable method of poisoning with good results. But on open seas, fishing is dangerous and yields vary greatly. In the lagoon, where empirical knowledge is sufficient, no magic, rituals, or prayers are linked with the operation. On the high seas, however, with the danger and uncertainty, fishing is surrounded by magical and religious observances.

The theory goes far in explaining how religion meets universal needs of individuals. In all cultures men face the crises of birth, puberty, marriage, and death. Religions everywhere focus on one or more of these universals. Religious belief helps individuals through crises by stressing the positive side of social life. Malinowski goes on to point out that religion also functions to strengthen the bonds of human cohesion.

It was primarily the second English anthropologist, A. R. Radcliffe-Brown, who emphasized the importance religion has for society. His theory resembles Durkheim's, but he omits an account of origin and concentrates on the function of various religious practices. Rites, for instance, are explained as the "regulated symbolic expressions" of certain sentiments. An orderly social life depends upon agreement among members of a society. This agreement is achieved by sharing common sentiments. The specific *social* function of ritual is to regulate and transmit through generations the sentiments that form the basis of society.

The two interpretations are not contradictions but rather supplements. Malinowski stresses what religion does for the individual; Radcliffe-Brown looks at the function of religion for society. Using the work of both these theorists, Raymond Firth has synthesized much of current anthropological thought on the nature of religion. In a chapter of his book *Elements of Social Organization* he demonstrates the cultural context of religion and emphasizes the need to understand religious life within its particular social framework. Using advances made in psychology, Firth is able to be more explicit than Malinowski about the function of religion for the individual. He shows how the psychological processes of rationalism, projection, and identification frequently operate in religion. From such an approach he derives the following conclusions: religion provides a referent for the explanation of many human events that demand a meaning; social life provides solutions to problems with the natural environment.

However, social life has disadvantages. Rivalry, factionalism, and personal violence arise in society. Empirical social controls reduce some of this conflict—for instance, sorcery and witchcraft provide a more acceptable explanation of social failures than does human inadequacy. Further, such practices channel aggressive impulses in ways generally not disruptive to society.

Religion unites members under a common aegis, supplies principles of order, provides a frame of reference for attitudes toward nature, supports systems of authority, and stabilizes most social relations.

Besides clarifying earlier functional analysis, Firth adds that religion also functions in the expression of imagination and aesthetic feelings. He notes that some of the finest art is based on religion and that religious systems have promoted philosophy through humility and self-examination.

Summary

Study of the relationship between men and the supernatural has supplied concepts such as sacred and profane, mana, shaman, and priest. The social sciences brought to the analysis of religion an objectivity that allowed insight into the ways psychological processes operate in religion and showed how psychosomatic ailments may be part of these supernatural relations. The major contribution of anthropology was the relating of religion to society, to show how religion provides a framework for solving problems inherent in social life. Specifically, religion was seen as a means to reduce anxiety, as a way of rewarding approved behavior, and as a supply of common sentiment. It is impossible to imagine the existence of a society that lacked all symbolic solutions of a nonempirical nature.

Suggested Readings

Firth, Raymond, *Elements of Social Organization*. New York: Franklin Watts, Inc., 1951. Chapter VII is particularly recommended. It states clearly the functional theory of religion and summarizes the work of leading British social anthropoligists.

Hoebel, E. Adamson, *The Cheyenne*. New York: Holt, Rinehart & Winston, Inc., 1960. Although this book is a general ethnography, it contains much material that illustrates how ritual, myth, and other parts of religion support and integrate with the social structure. The Cheyenne materials illustrate the theories of Firth (above) in an actual way of life.

Lessa, William, and Evon Vogt, *Reader in Comparative Religion*. New York: Harper & Row, Publishers, 1958. This collection presents the ideas of most of the theorists discussed in this chapter. In another section contemporary anthropologists evaluate the early theory and describe present thought. Other sections offer detailed studies of such subjects as mana, taboo, totemism, shamans, and priests.

9

A PERSPECTIVE OF CULTURE

An introduction to anthropology's concept of culture generally comes as a shock to many persons. Anthropologists emphasize man's similarities with other primates; it is not pleasant to learn that there are so few differences between oneself and apes or monkeys. Indeed, comparative anatomy can show only quantitative, not qualitative differences, between a chimpanzee and *Homo sapiens*. Prehistory reveals that man's ancestors were even more apelike. Also distressing is the fact that once a primate became man, a toolmaker, it took him several hundred thousand years to modify his simple stone tools.

As one studies the many contemporary cultures, one is struck by the great diversity of behavior, and the person who goes to live among another people is likely to experience a "cultural shock." Everyone begins learning at birth; much of this early learning becomes so ingrained that it is assumed to be "only natural." What one eats, wears, and believes soon becomes *the* way of eating, dressing, and believing. Therefore, it is upsetting to find other peoples who behave or believe differently. The easy assumption is that something is wrong with them; they will change rapidly once exposed to the "right" (our) way of doing things. Of course, their way is as natural to them as our way is to us.

145

Differences among cultures have been emphasized in the past by anthropologists. Early social evolutionists used the differences to indicate the various stages man had passed through in his evolutionary process. Students of diffusion and historical anthropologists tended to explain culture on the basis of unique historical events. Such an emphasis logically concentrates on particular differences. Early functional anthropologists saw cultures as whole systems adapting to their environments. Again logically, different environments would yield contrasting cultures.

Despite this background, cultural similarities were apparent throughout anthropology's history, and theorists grappled with explaining them in various ways. For instance, some historicalists overemphasized diffusion and attempted to trace all similarities to a common source. A few anthropologists, turning to psychology, postulated common instincts or a psychic unity of mankind. None of their theories was satisfactory, but attention was called to universal similarities.

The existence of similarities is a perplexing problem because anthropologists see man as a remarkably flexible creature. The newborn infant of *Homo sapiens* seems to be relatively free of the instincts or drives that determine much of the behavior in other species. Here is an organism with great potential for learning; the learning can mold it in almost any direction. Given the vast differences in time and space that separate peoples of the world, one would expect many different patterns of learning, producing many unique patterns of behavior.

Yet the preceding chapters should have made clear the many similarities among all cultures. A partial listing of cultural universals emphasizes these similarities among men: in relation to environment—body ornaments, cooking, decorative art, feasting, food taboos, housing; in relation to groups—age-grading, community organization, courtship, division of labor, education, family, government, incest taboos, inheritance rules, kin groups, kinship nomenclature, language, marriage, property rights, residence rules, status differentiation; in relation to the supernatural—folklore, funeral rites, magic, mourning, religious ritual, and soul concepts. Other universals include such specific items as music, dream interpretation, personal names, and surgery. These similarities are only a few among those listed in the Human Relations Area Files, an inventory of the world's cultures.

Of course, specific practices vary within some of these universals. That is, residence rules may specify that a couple live with the groom's family, the bride's family, or independently. These divergencies are at first striking and are worthy of investigation. In general, however, the important question concerns the universality of such rules. What is it about man that has led him into so many similar practices?

This question seems fundamental for all the behavioral sciences, and answers to it will doubtless provide a general theory of human behavior. Present answers are inadequate, but the similarity must lie in the nature of man's biology and psychology and the dynamics of group life. Physical anthropology provides some understanding of the biological life, psychology of the psychological, and sociology and cultural anthropology of group life. These fields do not explore separate sectors independently. Only continual cooperation of the disciplines will yield satisfactory solutions.

In the realms of the biological and psychological, early instinct theory has been discarded. To some extent "drives" or "impulses" are simply substitutes for instincts, but the use of these new terms generally is limited to such obvious needs as food, excretion, and avoidance of pain. Thus housing, as a universal, could be ascribed to the avoidance of pain. However, it is most difficult to ascribe such customs as residence rules or status differentiation to any genetic predisposition of man.

Another explanation from biology, which might be called a principle of limited possibilities, has to do with man's physiological capabilities. Childbirth, for instance, closely affiliates mother and infant. Even though the father may practice the couvade, the child remains dependent on the mother for food and care. In modern hospitals, infants are no longer denied human contacts in the name of sterility; caressing and holding are also important for health. The child's long dependency period thrusts him into social relations, and it probably is basic in man's being a social animal. Other phenomena, such as menstruation, sickness, and even breathing have brought common cultural responses.

A third explanation for similarities lies in the learning process. Enculturation is effective because of its symbolic nature, particularly the symbolism of language. The use of symbols sets man far apart from the other animals. Although the symbols vary greatly in their meaning, their use produces likenesses. The fact that all men symbolize must account not only for the universality of language but also in part for the universal development of religion with all its symbolism.

Further similarities in religion and also in government seem to derive from the common grounds of family life. The ways in which family members interact (and these forms of interaction are limited) are extended to the supernatural and to the state. The gods, for instance, are regularly treated in the ways in which one man treats another. Sacrifice can be seen as an extension of gift giving, laudation as a form of flattery, and prayer as a kind of begging or beseeching. It is no surprise that a god is often envisioned as a father or that relations with the supernational are often cast in terms of the family.

Finally, diffusion may account for some of the more perplexing similarities that cannot be accounted for otherwise. Although some anthropologists overemphasized diffusion, most people are unaware of how important it has been. An average American, for instance, would perhaps be shocked by the "foreign influence" at his breakfast table. His canteloupe was domesticated in Persia, his bacon and eggs a contribution from Southeast Asia, and his coffee an Arabic invention. The fork he uses originated in medieval Italy, and his spoon came from the Romans. The cotton in his tablecloth was first developed in India. If his wife (the origin of marriage undetermined) also served him cornflakes, then he can lay claim to one American discovery, corn having been raised by American Indians.

Painstaking work by earlier anthropologists has documented the extent of diffusion in recent times. Analysis of the distribution of traits and intensive use of historical documents give insight into the many similarities that exist because of borrowing. However, anthropologists have no way of knowing what common traits have persisted and spread since the time of early man. Further advances in prehistory will probably show other traits with one common origin. However, it will be extremely difficult to discover if some belief, such as the incest regulation, originated in the Paleolithic and simply continued. Anthropologists in the past were tempted to explain away similarities by diffusion, but their excessive reliance on the process should not blind future scientists to the potential of diffusion in producing universals of behavior.

It is the universal similarities among men that make a science of man possible. Social scientists are much more impressed with peoples' likenesses than with their differences. The regular, recurrent practices found in all cultures form the basis for the analysis of culture. Anthropology, with its resources for cross-cultural comparison, is responsible for clarifying the similarities. Joined with its sister sciences of psychology and sociology, the three must explain why the similarities exist. An understanding of why there are similarities is only beginning; a full understanding depends upon future work in the behavioral sciences.

INDEX